THE CROWNED
WHITE EAGLE

THE CROWNED WHITE EAGLE

My Polish Legacy

Anthony P. Kowalski

To order additional copies of this book, contact:
Xlibris Corporation
1-888-795-4274
www.Xlibris.com
Orders@Xlibris.com

CONTENTS

flag, sang patriotic songs, and strongly supported our American troops, then fighting with our Allied partners against the feared Axis powers. Mindful of the suffering of our Polish relatives, we also sang the Polish national anthem with its doleful opening line—"Poland is not yet lost, as long as we live!"[1]

Toward the end of our grammar school years, my classmates and I persuaded our pastor, Monsignor Lipinski, to sponsor a soccer team in the fifteen-year-old city league. We were proud not only to play on an organized ball team for the first time but also to wear maroon jerseys proclaiming us to be the St. Hedwig's Eagles. We played our games at the Extension Ball Field in North Trenton, which eventually became a shopping center. From St. Hedwig's I went on to Trenton Catholic Boys High School in South Trenton, and I was able to continue my soccer playing there.

As I completed my high school studies, the choice of college faced me. I had always done well academically, so my older siblings encouraged me to consider further studies, even though none of them had been permitted to do so. I was the youngest of six. College seemed a far-off dream.

During my senior year, our guidance counselor, Franciscan Fr. Casimir Sabol, summoned me and indicated that I was eligible for a four-year scholarship at a local Catholic college. I thought it over but declined the offer. I had previously discussed the matter with my pastor and indicated to him my desire to study Polish language and culture and work in the Polish-American community. He encouraged me to study at his alma mater, St. Mary's College, in Orchard Lake, Michigan. I was eager to do so.

Because of my refusal of the initial offer and the need of our family, Fr. Sabol assisted me in securing other financial scholarships. One was

---

1   *Jeszcze Polska nie zginęła,*

provided by the local newspaper—the Trenton Times Scholarship. Another was provided by the local Polish Arts Club of Trenton. With those two cash awards, supplemented by financial assistance from my family, I set off for St. Mary's in Orchard Lake, Michigan. After two years, my college career was interrupted by a five month stay in a TB sanitorium. I was able to return and complete my final two years at this Polish-American college. Never have I regretted my serious dedication to the Polish language and culture.

In the 1950s when I studied, few colleges existed in the United States where one could secure a good grounding in the Polish language and culture. Since then, unfortunately all have either closed—Alliance (PA) and St. Mary's (MI)—or have undergone significant changes in curriculum and student body—Madonna (MI), Nazareth (PA), and Felician (NJ). Such study nevertheless is available at some of the larger universities. I was therefore delighted when in the late nineties my only son, John, chose to study Polish in his undergraduate program at Harvard, followed by a summer immersed in Polish culture at the Jagiellonian, Poland's premier university, in Cracow. The interest in Poland, I'm happy to say, lives on. And the journey to discover those precious stories has persisted.

I

POLAND

The story of my family is inseparable from the history of the Polish people. From my earliest years I thrilled to tales Mother and others told about life in the old country—the small village, the hardy people, the farming and beekeeping, and the neighboring shrines and wayside chapels. A spirit of awe and reverence accompanied for me the mere mention of the word Poland.

Embellished with rituals and songs, the legends grew and the stories multiplied. An idyllic world emerged. I learned the legend of brothers Lech, Czech, and Rus about the origins of the Slavic states. Poles are considered the descendants of Lech. I envisioned a once-flourishing nation savaged by violent wars, a people who were not a nation except in their hearts and in their dreams. That world and its images I inherited, and as long as I lived, it would cast a spell over me.

In AD 966, Mieszko (MYESH-ko), a warrior of the Polanie tribe, succeeded in uniting the West Slavic tribes then wandering the fields of the Vistula River region in eastern Europe. The Polish word for field is pole (POE-le), hence the name by which they would ever be known. By consolidating power, Mieszko succeeded in strengthening these people from the perennial marauders from the west and from the east. He entered into a treaty with Otto I, head of the Holy Roman Empire, who officially recognized him as duke of Poland and friend of the emperor. Security seemed thereby attained.

Realizing that he would need to either adopt Christianity or be pressured to do so, he wisely turned not to Byzantium in the east nor to the Germans in the west but to Slavic neighbors in the south. He chose to marry the Bohemian princess Dubravka and become baptized with all his subjects. He furthermore gave all his lands into the hands of the Holy See, making it part of the patrimony of Peter, thus placing it under papal protection. This would provide solid support through some of the gravest crises Poland would endure in later centuries.

It was Mieszko's eldest son and successor, Bolesław (Bol-LES-wav) the Brave, who would be crowned the first king of Poland in 1025. The German emperor, Otto III, in agreement with Pope Silvester II and in pursuit of a Christian world order, sanctioned the establishment of a metropolitan see in Gniezno (GNYEZH-no) with several bishoprics dependent on it. He also placed his crown on the head of Bolesław and presented him with the lance of St. Maurice, a symbol of royalty. The Piast dynasty, so revered among the Polish people, would endure for many centuries.

Otto III's vision of a federation of Christian monarchs united in their allegiance to the emperor and the pope was abandoned by his successors. They repeatedly sought German expansion to the east. Poles maintained the support of Rome, which itself struggled to retain control over ecclesiastical administration throughout the empire. A relentless series of conflicts ensued.

The Polish nation, nevertheless, grew and thrived under some outstanding kings, like Casimir the Great (1310–70), who "inherited a Poland of wood and bequeathed one of stone"; like Jagiełło (Ya-GYE-wo) (1386–1434), the Lithuanian prince who married Queen Hedwig and wisely managed both kingdoms, leading the nation to its greatest expansion in size and glory; and like John Sobieski (1674–96), who saved western civilization by defeating the Turks at Vienna. The road to progress seemed secure, but all came to a tragic end in the late eighteenth century.

The Partitions of Poland, 1772, 1793, 1795. (From Davies, Norman, *God's Playground - A History of Poland*, New York: Columbia Univ. Press, 1982, Vol. I, 512)

Because Poles lacked natural borders other than the Baltic Sea in the north and the Tatra Mountains in the south, neighbors repeatedly attacked them, both from the east and from the west. Wedged between Germany and Russia, Poland's history is framed by constant battles with its neighbors. As a result, Polish boundaries were constantly altered. And after eight centuries of freedom and prosperity came two centuries of barbaric occupation and repression.

In the late eighteenth century, Poles, like the Americans, craved freedom. On March 4,1789, the United States adopted its constitution, proclaiming independence and sovereignty; on May 3, 1791, Poland did the same. But the destiny of each veered differently. The former started a new nation on the road to freedom and democracy, growth and prosperity; the latter spawned alarm among neighboring sovereigns, who feared those initiatives would spread into their domains. This led to joint intervention, resulting in the annihilation of the Polish state and the subjugation of its people.

The superpowers—Russia, Prussia, and Austria—would not tolerate democracy and freedom. They agreed among themselves that allowing such a development next door would pose a threat to their sovereignty. If such a movement succeeded, their peoples might demand the same and agitate to overthrow them. They therefore connived to wipe out this potential threat to their sovereign rule.

In three successive partitions—1772, 1793, and 1795—the superpowers of the day carved up Poland's lands among themselves. For the next two centuries, Poles were subject to foreign overlords. The western lands were taken over by Prussians, the southern lands by Austro-Hungarians, and the eastern lands by Russians. Not until after World War I did Poland regain its independence, but even that freedom was short-lived. Hitler had other plans.

The 1930s saw the rise of the greatest military machine the world had ever seen. Nazi Germany created a massive force of tanks, cannons, aircraft, and highly trained army and, on September 1, 1939, in collusion with Stalin's forces in Russia, unleashed a blitzkrieg, a lightning strike on Poland. Like a jackal springing on its prey, this immense Nazi war machine pounced on its neighbor. Within two weeks it was all over.

Western Poland lay writhing in the claws of the jackal, and Stalin moved his troops into eastern Poland.

(anatolisgmesroom.blogspot.com)

The Nazis immediately closed all colleges, universities, and seminaries, killing off university professors and professionals from all walks of life, including military leaders and outspoken clergy. Nothing more than a trade school education was permitted to the citizenry. Nazi troops shipped young women to assist as servants in German families whose masters were at the front. They sent young men to hard work in the factories in support of the war effort.

Unlike what they would later do when they invaded France and installed a puppet government, the Nazis refused to allow in Poland any form of self-rule. From the very beginning their intent was enslavement and subjugation. As Czeslaw Milosz, the Nobel Laureate, noted:

> ... the German occupation of France was fundamentally different from the occupation of Poland. It is possible that this can be explained by the German inferiority complex with regard to French culture and their contempt for the "subhumans" to the east of Germany.[2]

Western Poles became subject to German overlords. Nazi generals were placed in charge of different regions of the country and ruled with unremitting terror. In the five succeeding years, Nazis murdered six million Polish citizens—half of them Jews, half Catholics. Polish Jewry was annihilated in an unprecedented holocaust. The rich Yiddish heritage of music and song, theatre, and entertainment was wiped out in one diabolic orgy of hatred.

The Russians were no less barbaric in eastern Poland. Stalin ordered 1.6 million Poles removed from their homes and shipped off mostly to the Siberian tundra as slave laborers, never again to see their homeland. Many died along the way; others expired in captivity under grotesquely inhumane conditions. Some descendants survive to this day, deprived of all that their families held dear.

Stalin also ordered the execution of over 15,000 defenseless Polish military officers. Each was shot with a single bullet to the back of the head and buried secretly in the Katyn Forest. The media were kept unaware of these events.

It was not long before Hitler, in his mad grab for power, turned against the Russians in June 1941. In subsequent warfare, the Germans

---

2   Czesław Miłosz. *A Year of the Hunter,* trans, Madeline G. Levine (New York: Farrar. Straus and Giroux, 1994), 275.

in 1943 came upon the Katyn burial site, and their propaganda machine publicized this extensively as a major example of Stalin's barbaric policies. The Russian government initially denied its involvement and sought to blame the Germans. The horrid truth is now well known and documented—Stalin had given the order.

Almost fifty years later, in 1990, the Russian government finally acknowledged the lie. A memorandum from the head of the NKVD, Lavrenti Beria, to Joseph Stalin, dated March 1940 was revealed. It recommended "death by shooting" to 14,700 people held in POW camps (including Polish officers and soldiers), as well as 11,000 people held in prisons in the Ukraine and Belarussia. Diagonally across the page are the signatures of Stalin, Voroshilov, Molotov, and Mikoyan, and in the margins the signatures of Comrades Kalinin and Kaganovich. Poles have always known the truth.

After Hitler's attack on Russia in 1941, the Russian armies joined with the allies in an effort to destroy the German war machine. United Allied forces gradually gained strength and relentlessly pursued the Nazi terrorists. American and British troops pushed forward through western Europe, liberating Paris in August 1944. Stalin's forces similarly advanced deep into Polish territory and quickly reached the Vistula River opposite Warsaw. But here the liberation of Poland's capital city would take another tragic turn.

Poland's underground army attacked German forces in Warsaw and initially made some progress. They had hoped to forestall Russian control and establish a base for an independent Polish government. In vain did they seek help from the Allies. Stalin controlled all access routes to Warsaw, effectively blocking western support to the freedom fighters. He simply waited with his troops outside Warsaw until Hitler regrouped his forces and with overwhelming strength crushed the insurgents and the civilian population.

The Polish freedom fighters fought heroically but ultimately had to surrender. Hitler deported the remaining citizenry and leveled every building left standing in the capital. A city of 1,250,000 before the war was left a pile of rubble, without a single inhabitant. Only then did Stalin's troops march in. They would subsequently call themselves "liberators" of the Polish people!

Before departing from Poland, Nazi forces bombed almost everything in sight, leaving Warsaw, the capital of the Polish nation, in total rubble. Despite desperate cries for assistance from Polish freedom fighters, American and British forces would not intervene. Stalin demanded nonintervention as the price of his support of the Allies. The memory of Russian callousness and Allied nonintervention in deference to Stalin remains deeply ingrained in Polish consciousness.

The aftermath of the war was again grotesquely unfair. Two-thirds of the German citizenry, which had supported these monstrously criminal atrocities, were granted freedom, democracy, self-government, and—through the Marshall Plan—millions of dollars to help them rebuild their cities. In contrast, all the tortured and penurious victims in eastern Europe were condemned to further enslavement, this time under an alien, atheistic, Communist ideology, without freedom, without democracy, and under a puppet government. Lost too was the possibility of massive rebuilding through the Marshall Plan. Stalin would not allow it.

In the post–World War II territorial shift, Russia took over large portions of what belonged to Poland prior to the war. At the same time, they ceded to Poland portions of German-occupied territories, which had earlier belonged to Poland. The map of Poland was again changed.

The Polish people would have to wait another forty-four years before regaining their long sought freedom and democracy. By then, the original aggressors to the west were once again strong and powerful; and the original aggressors to the east, also strong and powerful, withdrew their troops so that they might better concentrate on their own reforms. But Poland lay in poverty and ruin. Five decades of satanic bloodsucking—first by Nazis, then by Communists—had taken their toll.

Post World War II Territorial Shifts, from Library of Congress, Historical Maps of Poland.

Two centuries of infamy have been inflicted on the Polish people. In the course of their suffering they have been inspired by several notable personages:

- a man who captured in music the yearnings and the passion of the Polish people—Fryderyk Chopin;
- a woman physicist who discovered radium and opened the door to a new era of medical knowledge and treatment of disease—*Marya Skłodowska*, better known as Madame Curie;

- an electrician who lit the spark that ignited a revolution, leading to the fall of the Berlin Wall and the crumbling of Communism throughout the Slavic world—*Lech Wałęsa* (Va-WEN-sa);
- a priest who endured Nazi cruelty and Communist repression to rise up on the world stage and proclaim a message of hope and triumph over tyranny—*Karol Wojtyła* (Voy-TI-wa), better known as Pope John Paul II.

These noble sons and daughters of Poland have sustained and inspired the people through two centuries of occupation and devastation. One of the most patriotic Polish hymns, Rota, captures the sentiment of the Polish people. Written in 1910 and banned by subsequent oppressors, it will always ring true in the hearts of Poles everywhere:

"Never will we abandon our ancestral land,
Nor allow our language to be suppressed.
We are the Polish nation, the Polish people,
Descended from the royal line of Piast.
Never again shall the enemy oppress us,
So help us God! So help us God!"

II

THE BUSINESS CARD

In the post–World War II days, because Dad never owned a car, we traveled everywhere on foot—to church, to market, to cemetery. All were located within a two-mile radius. If needed, the Trenton Transit bus system could transport us to more distant places. That meant occasionally shopping downtown in the fancier stores or going to the cathedral for special celebrations. But those opportunities were rare.

At age fifteen, I ambled along with Mother to Aunt Victoria's house. She was married to my father's uncle, Joseph Kowalski. Daily for several years I had trudged along that same one-mile path to serve Mass, to attend school, to visit relatives. Up and over the Olden Avenue Bridge we would climb with the wind at our back, then downhill, only to be faced with another uphill trek toward our twin-steeple parish church in the distance—St. Hedwig's.

Distinctive fragrances and sounds accompanied the journey. We passed Maziarz's Fruit Stand with luscious fruits and vegetables laid out on the sidewalk; Pazdan's Poultry Market with fetid chicken coops and screeching poultry; Eagle Bakery with its fragrant pastries and breads; Polish Falcons' Hall reeking of alcohol from its well-stocked bar and resonating with strikes from its bowling alleys; and finally the St. Hedwig's complex—a grammar school with a large convent next to it and a large Gothic church with a rectory alongside. On a side street just before the school and across from the convent stood my grandaunt's home.

Aunt Victoria's house was located in North Trenton, which we then considered a more upscale residential area compared to our East Trenton haunts. A canal and railroad yard separated North Trenton from East Trenton. The only access to each lay over the Olden Avenue Bridge, crowned with a massive steel structure from which vessels could be viewed and the drawbridge lifted to allow access on the canal below. I never saw the drawbridge drawn. By the forties, all travel on the canal had ceased, and by the fifties, the canal was no longer visible. The city had erected a highway bypass atop the canal bed, so the steel drawbridge became useless clutter.

On one particular journey with my mother, I listened attentively as she prepared me for meeting my aged aunt. She began telling me about my ancestors. My grandparents, John and Antoinette Kowalski, had migrated from Poland at the end of the nineteenth century and settled in East Trenton. Aunt Victoria married grandfather's younger brother, Joseph. Now an octogenarian, she was the last survivor of that generation. Like the others, she spoke only Polish. We referred to her as Stryjenka (stree-YEN-kah), meaning paternal aunt; she in turn called me Antoś (AHN-tosh), the equivalent of Tony.

Mother showed great deference to her in-laws. This was due as much to her inbred respect for the elderly as to her naturally warm and courteous disposition. She had no close family in America, so her husband's relatives became her own. Like them, she had emigrated from Poland in her youth and still retained fond memories of Polish farmlands, family customs, and religious practices. She and Stryjenka held much in common.

The lengthy conversations between Mother and Grandaunt had little appeal to me. They would discuss activities at church, people in the community, and the condition of each other's health. Then, as so frequently happens with old-timers, they once again recalled the past. The current wretched conditions in post–World War II Poland in contrast to glorious days gone by played again and again. My mind wandered. They lived, it seemed, in another world.

After a while Mother said, "Stryjenka, tell Antoś about the village of the Kowalskis in Poland. I'm sure he'd like to hear about that." This aroused my interest, as Mother knew it would. Dad had recently died. Although his wife, father, and mother and all his uncles and aunts as young adults had migrated from Poland, Dad had spent his entire life in his beloved New Jersey. Rarely did he travel beyond it. Nevertheless, he cherished all that pertained to his ancestral land and conveyed the same reverence to me. Having recently viewed his grave and the other family plots in St. Hedwig's Cemetery, I was keenly interested in our origins. I turned to my aunt and pleaded with her to go on.

"Oh, my mind is not clear anymore," she said, feigning indifference. But seeing my aroused curiosity, she soon began. "Well, it was like this. My Joe and your grandfather, John, were brothers. With their sisters Mary and Frances, they settled in this area around 1890. One other brother, Val, also joined them, but he went on to Scranton. They all came from the region of Poznan. We called them Prusaki (Prue-SAH-key) because that region of Poland was then part of Prussia. Your grandfather even served in the Prussian Army. He was a striking figure."

"Oh, yes," Mother interrupted, "I remember him marching in parades with the local Polish fraternal organization. He stood ramrod straight, a large man at least six feet tall. With his thick mustache, he looked like a typical Prussian soldier. In fact, his friends nicknamed him Kaiser because of his striking resemblance to the Prussian leader. But please go on, Stryjenka."

"The village was located several kilometers from the city of Poznan. Nearby were the towns Pyzdry (PIZZ-dree), Środa (SHROE-dah), and Żerkow (ZHER-koff). The Warta (VAR-ta) River flowed not far away. And farther down lay Jarocin (Ya-ROH-cheen), the largest town in the region. The Kowalskis visited it often. All of those places, mind you, were in Greater Poland, called Wielkopolska (VYEL-ko-POL-ska), the oldest region in Poland, of which Poznan is the chief city. I know the names don't mean much to you now, Antoś, but maybe someday they will."

"And what about the village itself, Stryjenka? What was it like?" I asked.

"Very small," she responded. "Maybe twenty or thirty families according to your Uncle Joe. That's all."

"And the name of the village?"

"They referred to it as Antonin (An-TOH-neen)."

"Wait a minute, please, Stryjenka." I turned to my mother for pencil and paper. She scoured through her purse and finally came up with an old business card and a red pencil. Reversing the card to the unprinted side, I prepared to write. "Okay, Stryjenka, please, how do you spell that?"

"Oh, I'm not sure," she said, somewhat embarrassed.

Mother then helped. "That's A-N-T-O-N-I-N. You must remember that name when you grow up, Antoś." Turning to my grandaunt, she said, "I do think someday he will find it, Stryjenka. Thanks to you."

"I hope so, Mom" I said. "And please give me the names again of each of those nearby towns." I wrote them down as Mom spelled them out for me. "Thank you, very much, Stryjenka" I said.

She patted me on the head. "Oh, if only your grandfather had lived to see you. That old Prussian would be so proud to know that you're interested in his little village!"

I pocketed the card and smiled as we exchanged our farewell. "Do widzenia" (Doh vee-DSE'-nya).

On our way home, I turned to my mother and inquired, "What about the village you came from, Mom? Can you tell me about that?"

"Oh, some other time, Antoś. It's not that important."

"But I want to know about that place too, Mom. Someday I'd like to visit there," I said.

"Some other time," she repeated.

I placed the small business card in my wallet, where it remained for many years. When one wallet wore out, I transferred its contents to another. Together with my Selective Service Form and Social Security Number, the card would accompany me everywhere. Stashed away, it was rarely viewed. Not until four decades later …

III

THE KOWALSKIS

For many years, I carried around with me the business card, which held the identity of my paternal ancestral village. It would be my link to the past. But before searching for that village abroad, I needed to be clear about the Kowalski trail on this side of the Atlantic. As the youngest in a family of six children, I was less acquainted than my siblings with the older generation. Perhaps more inquisitive than most, I pursued relentlessly with questions the few elderly who remained—chiefly my mother but also uncles, aunts, and distant cousins. From such inquiries I pieced together much of the story.

At all times my paternal grandmother, Antoinette Kubis Kowalski—a short stocky woman with Slavic cheekbones, braided hair, and fierce determination—exhibited toward me a gentle warmth. She was the only grandparent I ever knew. My earliest recollections are of a strong-willed woman who would walk great distances alone—trudging along the mile or so to church or the half mile to the shopping center, carrying her large, heavy purse and maybe even a few packages as well. We called her Babcia (BAB-cha), meaning Granny.

I loved to go to Babcia's house because she would always have something for me, usually candy or sweets. When ill, I could always count on her to show up with a can of fruit cocktail and insist that I eat a large portion. I didn't like the syrupy taste; it oozed with sugary sweetness. But I drank it anyway. On cold winter nights, after walking through the freezing snow to get to her house, I could also count on a small taste of wine or brandy "to warm my insides" as she would say. I did enjoy that!

My grandparents, Jan and Antonina Kubis Kowalski, c. 1928

My grandmother, Babcia Kowalski, died at seventy-six when I was thirteen. From my vantage point then, she seemed much older; from my perspective today around the same age, not old at all. Too soon did breast cancer destroy her. I recall being ushered out of the room as my grandmother revealed the horrible disfigurement of her breast to my older sisters with a warning that they take care of themselves so that the same would not happen to them. She would speak almost religiously of her St. Joseph's salve, which provided her much comfort. Because of her religious bent, I assumed that it had some miraculous powers through the intercession of that saint. Only later did I learn it was a normal skin salve made in St. Joseph, Missouri.

Of her early life I know very little, neither her place of birth nor the size of her family. She apparently came from the same area as my grandfather, the Poznan region, and arrived on this continent two years after him, in 1892. As far as we can determine, she had three sisters in America. Each assimilated rapidly into the American environment. One married a Matulewicz and lived in Wisconsin; their offspring took the name Mathews. Another married a Surdukowski and lived in Whiting, Indiana; their progeny shortened the name to Surd or Surdy. A third sister married a Piteleski in Ohio, and their offspring became Poliskeys. Thus took place a thorough Anglicization of the names of my cousins. In contrast, we Kowalskis kept intact our original spelling.

One of the offspring of our Ohio relatives was John "Bull" Poliskey, star of a 1927 Notre Dame football team coached by Knute Rockne. Uncle Pete attended one of those contests and shared with the family a glowing account about his cousin. We kept at home a memento of that event—a game program. Most Catholics foster a special fondness for Notre Dame, but because of our family connection with Rockne and Poliskey, we Kowalskis had an additional reason for pride in the Fighting Irish.

I was able to gather much more information about my grandfather Jan Kowalski. We referred to him as Dziadek (JAH-dek), meaning Grandpa. The 1920 census records indicate that he arrived in America in

1890 and became a naturalized citizen five years later. After working in the mills around Trenton, he died in 1930, four years before I was born. I knew his brother Joseph in Trenton and his sister Mary Kurzawa in South Amboy. Each treated me royally. Another brother, Valentine, lived in Scranton and another sister, Frances, in Trenton. Both predeceased my birth. All five of them, I learned, emigrated from that same small village in Prussian Poland.

Dziadek, it appears, visited his brother Walenty (Valentine) in Scranton at the turn of the century, during a rebellion of Polish Catholics against their bishop. Such conflicts in those days were common between the mostly Irish, English-speaking bishops and the foreign-speaking immigrant communities, which sought to preserve their language and customs. In Scranton, the conflict resulted in a severe rupture in the Polish-American community. As told to me, one side remained loyal to the bishop and pastor; the other lined up with the assistant pastor, Hodur. This young priest later gained episcopal consecration by an Old Catholic bishop in the Netherlands and established many other parishes among the Polish immigrant communities. The group became known as the Polish National Church and now numbers several dioceses in America and in Poland.

Grandfather never joined the dissidents, but instead returned to Trenton and remained a Roman Catholic. His brother Walenty, however, sided with Hodur. As time went on, our families unfortunately failed to keep contact. My attempts in later years to find relatives in Pennsylvania have been unsuccessful.

Dad was born into the community of recently arrived Polish immigrants in New Jersey in 1898. He spent his entire life in the same neighborhood of East Trenton. He and his three brothers were called the four bears, though only Uncle John, the oldest, had the large bearlike physique, which warranted that name. A picture of their joint First Holy Communion depicts three of them together—John, the oldest, barrel-chested and chubby; Frank, handsome and athletic, soon to be a local soccer star; and Anthony, my Dad, the youngest of the three. A younger brother, Peter, not in the picture, was yet a toddler. Two younger sisters, Josephine Dymnicki and Helen Biesiada, rounded out the family.

During World War I, Dad's two older brothers were drafted and became doughboys in the American army. In the heat of battle, Uncle John endured a gunshot wound in the arm, but survived. Uncle Frank, however, was killed. They fought in France while struggling against the very Prussian troops with which their father once marched. Because of those events, my grandparents appealed to the draft board not to take their third son, my father, claiming that they needed him at home. To his chagrin and lifelong regret, Dad never served in the military. He nevertheless took great pride in his brothers' sacrifices during World War I and in his son Tom's later service with the Flying Tigers during World War II. But being staunchly patriotic, he always regretted not having fought himself.

My parents, Anthony and
Mary Padykula Kowalski, 1947.

Dad's formal education ended after the fourth grade when his parents removed him from school and sent him off to work in a factory. Years later my parents met Dad's fourth-grade teacher who told him, "One of my saddest days in teaching was the day they took you out of school." Evidently he had shown much ability and promise. His parents, however, considered work more important than schooling. They therefore entered him into the labor force as soon as possible. He never was given the opportunity to further his education.

In his younger years, Dad once mentioned to his mother that he would like to be a priest. She laughed at him saying, "There's no money available for idle dreams like that." So Dad put aside those aspirations and undertook a life of hard physical labor. He became a "dipper" of toilets and tubs at the local pottery. The factory was not yet mechanized, so his job required that he physically lift each piece into the dip and then hoist it away, drenching himself with glaze in the process. He worked at that job for many years before mechanization and the assembly line did away with his position.

Dad's marriage at twenty-one proved a blessing. With a devoted wife and a good-paying job, he secured a modest home for his family, and they initially prospered. Four children arrived rapidly—Veronica in 1921, Thomas in 1922, Irene in 1925, and Jean in 1927. Then came the Depression. With four children to support, Dad faced the ravages of that period jobless and without income. Around the same time, his younger brother, Peter, died at twenty-three of a stomach ailment, which, I am told, could have been treated routinely if proper medical care was available and affordable. Soon thereafter in 1932 at the height of the Depression and in the midst of their greatest poverty my sister, Marie, was born.

Relatives and neighbors fortunately came to my parents' rescue in their poverty. Both Mr. Eleniewski, the milkman, and Mr. Tarnowski, the local grocer, extended credit to my parents for several years, enabling them to have food for the family. After the Depression, it took some time but eventually my parents paid off all their bills. The Eleniewskis and Tarnowskis became our lifelong friends. Dad finally gained employment in 1934 and, as prospects began to improve in 1934, I, the last of six, arrived on the scene.

Stories from those harsh years abounded in our family. At one time in the midst of his poverty, Dad applied for employment at one pottery shop. An unscrupulous doctor claimed that he detected heart trouble and rejected his application. As it turned out, the doctor had lied in order to secure the position for his friend. Never in his life did Dad experience heart problems. He eventually gained employment at Trenton Potteries and remained working there for the final sixteen years of his life.

One Christmas during the Depression, my parents had no resources with which to celebrate. They could afford neither gifts nor decorations. Mother fretted about how to observe Christmas fittingly with her children. Suddenly Dad's newly married youngest sister, Helen, appeared with her husband, Lou Biesiada. They held in their hands a Christmas tree and ornaments and gifts for all. The children's eyes gleamed with joy, and my mother's filled with tears. It was a gesture that our family long remembered.

Religious practices were woven into the pattern of Dad's life. Besides his rigorous fidelity to Sunday and Holy Day Mass attendance, Dad observed to the fullest all prescribed fasting and abstinence laws. We all remember him getting down on his knees to pray before going to bed every evening. He and Mother saw to our observing the same practices.

During the Forty Hours' Devotions, he and every member of the family took turns at different hours of the day and night in adoration before the Blessed Sacrament. Both sons, like their father and uncles before them, served as altar boys, while the girls were faithful members of the Sodality of the Blessed Virgin Mary. Dad belonged to the Holy Name Society and Mom to the Rosary Society.

Dad, moreover, observed some distinctly Polish customs as well. On Good Friday, for example, he would awaken children with the gentle stroke of a leather strap saying "Boże Rany" (BOH-zhe RAH-ny) meaning "Christ's Wounds." It reminded us of Christ's sufferings on that day. Then on Easter Monday morning while shouting "Dingus" (DEEN-goos), he would awaken all with a sprinkling of water, reminiscent of baptismal rebirth. For my mother it meant a full bucket of water while sleeping in bed! All the children delighted in these traditions which, though adopted from the pagan past, reflected fundamental Christian truths.

Dad's American patriotism was legendary. During the playing of the national anthem before the Friday night fights on radio, he would stand at attention. The Fourth of July and Memorial Day celebrations moreover had for us the aura of religious feasts. Flags and songs colored each event. With gusto Dad would sing from his patriotic repertoire—"Yankee Doodle Dandy," "America the Beautiful," and "She's a Grand Old Flag." He would also enthrall us with humorous ditties, which made us laugh, like "K-K-K-Katie" and "I'm Forever Blowing Bubbles." Also memorable in those days was the annual two-mile trek to the cemetery on Memorial Day. There Dad and I placed a flag on the grave of my Uncle Frank and paid respect at the graves of the rest of the family. Dad proudly showed an unabashed and unapologetic patriotism.

Anyone who knew him remembered the ever-present plug of tobacco in his cheek, and the packet of Beechnut Tobacco in his back pocket. Dad began chewing as a teenager while working in the pottery and continued the practice throughout his life. That tobacco, I'm told, provided some comfort amid the pottery dust that seeped into his lungs. Unfortunately in later years alcohol became a further catalyst. That combination of tobacco and alcohol and pottery dust, doctors now tell us, contributed to the esophageal cancer, which shortened his life.

Unable to drive a car, Dad journeyed only on rare occasions to New York or Philadelphia. Poland he never saw. After World War II, when life in the United States seemed to return to normalcy and Dad's life could at last become comfortable and secure, the scourge of cancer afflicted him. He died on March 8, 1950, at the age of fifty-two. As my sister Irene wrote, by way of eulogy, "With all the many adversities in his life, Dad never turned against God, never became embittered, never engaged in recriminations against anyone. Everyone who knew him had the highest respect for him, just as he himself respected one and all. Some might call him a loser. I am totally convinced that when Dad stood before the Lord, he was greeted with, 'Well done, good and faithful servant.' And after all, that's what it's all about."

Dad's life gave yet another example of the tyranny and injustice so frequently imposed on us in life. He lived longer than his three brothers—none lived beyond their early fifties—and deprived of education while forced to enter the labor force at an early age, he followed the same pattern of endurance as they. All of this was bequeathed as part of their Polish inheritance. That heritage is mine.

IV

MOTHER'S STORY

My earliest recollections are of my mother, Mary Padykula Kowalski. In later conversations with her, I pieced together her poignant story. Her father, Jan Padykuła, came to America in the late 1880s. Like thousands of other immigrants in that period, he was lured by the potential for wealth and prosperity. Often would Mother repeat, "In those days people believed that America's streets were paved with gold."

Initially grandfather worked at a mill in Sayerville, New Jersey. After experiencing periodic layoffs, he gathered his modest possessions and trudged with his pack on his back along the railroad tracks from Sayerville to Baltimore, a distance of more than 140 miles. He had heard that better jobs were available at the Baltimore Harbor, so he set off in that direction and walked the entire distance. He had hoped to establish his family in America.

Railroad tracks in that northeast corridor passed over large river expanses, including the Delaware and the Susquehanna. Halfway across one of these, he said, he spotted a train rapidly approaching from the opposite direction. Quickly he scampered underneath. Holding on to the trestle for what appeared to be an interminable period as the train passed over him, he then climbed back up to resume his journey. That episode with all its pathos has been told and retold in our family for several generations.

Grandfather secured employment at the Baltimore Harbor but not for long. A letter from Poland soon arrived, alerting him that his wife lay seriously ill. He immediately departed. Shortly after his return to Poland she died, leaving him with an infant son, Anthony. Grandfather subsequently remarried and from this second marriage to a much younger Catherine Sypek was born first a son, Joseph, and then in 1896 a daughter, Mary Catherine Padykula, my mother. Seven more children followed.

Mother grew up in a small village in southeastern Poland called Wadowice Górne (Vah-doe-VEE-tse GOOR-ne) in the province of Mielec (MYE-lets) then governed by Austria. As the eldest daughter, she served as substitute mother for her younger siblings. Rocking them to sleep, minding them when her mother went off to the market, and assisting with countless household chores, she spent a busy childhood as a surrogate mother amid loving family and friends.

Mother was particularly fond of her grandfather. It was a mutual love. She followed him around the yard as he tended the bees. He had a keen sense of humor and, realizing his granddaughter's fascination with his hobby, he amused her with his antics. From time to time, he would encourage her to dip her hand along the edge of the container of honey, then lick her fingers with delight as she savored the sweet-tasting nectar. The memory of that delicacy remained with her lifelong.

After her thirteenth birthday, this pleasant world became shattered. Her parents then revealed to her that they had decided that she should travel to America to live with an aunt whose daughter had recently died. Grandfather had never forgotten the wonders of America and planned to transfer gradually his entire family. Mother would be the first, followed shortly by his older son, Anthony.

Her initial reaction was joy and gratitude. This could be an exciting adventure. Little did she realize that never again would she see those she loved most—parents, grandparents, older brother Joseph, orthopedically impaired infant sister Sophie, and siblings and friends.

The journey to Hamburg was long and tedious—on foot, by wagon, by rail. For the first time Mother visited large cities and viewed wondrous automobiles. Airplanes were not yet known. Boarding the SS Pretoria, a ship of the Hamburg-American Lines, she set off for America in the company of a family from her native village, the Migas. Her parents had made arrangements for them to look after her on the journey. After the voyage, she would never again see members of the Miga family.

During that memorable journey, a charming and well-dressed woman befriended her. Often would she seek Mother out, converse with her, and cause her to laugh. Mother's village companions, however, strongly discouraged this friendship. She did not understand their behavior. Only later did she learn that the woman ran a brothel in New York City and was trying to lure Mother to that profession!

Seventy-five years later, at the National Archives in Washington, I perused the ship's manifest of that historic trip. Mother had indicated that the vessel had landed in New York Harbor on Good Friday in 1910. I soon deduced that that day fell on March 25. After securing in the archives the microfilm tape for that day, I placed it on the reader and reviewed the manifest of ship after ship until I came upon one from Hamburg. Many handwritten pages and smeared lines I scoured, searching for the names of Mother and her fellow villagers. My heart pounded as, with growing eagerness, I waded through page after page. At last a feeling of elation came over me. I leaned forward and kissed the entry.

Her name, Marya Padykuła, appeared with her age, names of parents, and village of birth. Country of origin was listed as Austria, because that section of partitioned Poland then fell under Austrian rule. One entry puzzled me. Her age was given as eleven, yet we know that she was thirteen. A hasty review of the entire ship's manifest disclosed the names of many other children eleven years of age, but none twelve or thirteen. The reason became clear. Fares in those days were half price for children under twelve!

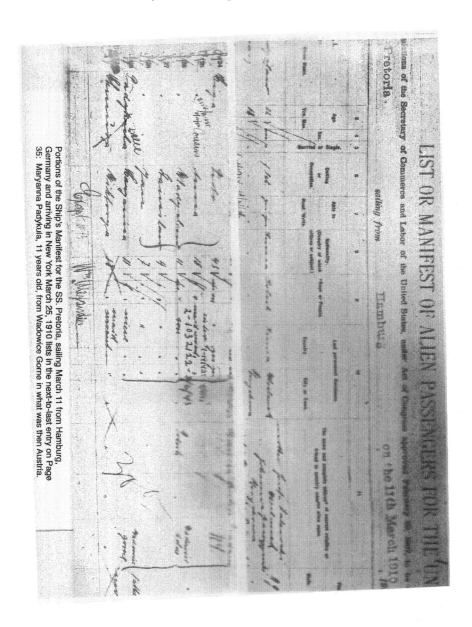

Portions of the Ship's Manifest for the SS. Pretoria, sailing March 11 from Hamburg, Germany and arriving in New York March 25, 1910 lists in the next-to-last entry on Page 35: Maryanna Padykula, 11 years old, from Wadowice Gorne in what was then Austria.

The journey over the ocean took several weeks. Mother spent her time aboard in very unfamiliar surroundings, wandering among a few fellow villagers whom she barely knew, an importunate madam who tried to solicit her, and curious strangers who could not communicate with her because of the language. Ignorance of English contributed to her isolation; the cold and murky weather did not help. After interminable days at sea, they spotted land and excitement spread rapidly among the passengers. They all ran to the guardrail with squeals of joy as they viewed the Iron Lady.

The SS Pretoria left Hamburg, Germany, on March 11, 1910, and reached the New York Harbor on Friday, March 25. Soon the passengers gathered their belongings and began to disembark, including the Miga family. Mother, however, was required to stay on board until someone claimed her. No one did. She was remanded to a waiting room until the dilemma could be solved. That entire weekend she remained on board in a waiting room.

For a while she felt happy that she might be returning to her parents. What wonderful stories of her journey would she tell them! But then on Easter Monday her aunt arrived, brusquely excusing herself because of the holidays. All businesses, she claimed, were closed, so she assumed that the dock would be also. Together they traveled the final phase of her journey to Trenton, New Jersey.

Details about Mother's life with her aunt are not clear. Initially, it seems, she was given the task of babysitting for neighborhood children as she had done in Poland. Her aunt, however, would not permit her to socialize with young people her age, preferring that she spend her time taking care of the children. This was a sad period in Mother's life. Her relationship with her aunt deteriorated rapidly. She had expected to go to school, but her aunt saw no value in that and prevented her from studying. Feeling homesick and unloved, she yearned for her family across the ocean.

Fortunately Mother knew of a cousin in Providence, Rhode Island, not much older than she. Secretly she wrote to her and shared her plight. The cousin, Mary Lonczak, and her husband encouraged her to leave her aunt in Trenton and come to stay with them in Providence. And so, in a fit of frustration one day, she gathered her meager belongings and traveled by train to New York and then to Providence—a bold move for a teenager who spoke little English and was unaccustomed to travel in America. She could barely pronounce the name of the city to which she was heading. "Prrro-vee-DEN-tse Errr-eee," she told the conductor, pointing to the words spelled out on an envelope. He guided her safely to Rhode Island.

Her cousin had recently married. The newlyweds welcomed Mother warmly and gave her the kindness and love she needed. A short time later, Mother received a scolding letter from her parents in Poland berating her for abandoning her aunt. The aunt had written a negative letter, complaining about her. This devastated Mother. Mary Lonczak consoled her and then wrote back to Mother's parents an accurate account of events as she perceived them. Her parents thereafter responded with love and understanding. Mother always retained a fondness and deep respect for the Lonczaks for providing help when most needed.

It became a family joke in later years to refer to Mother humorously as a teenage runaway. While amused by our humor, she could not bring herself to laugh. It was painfully obvious that she had gone through a terrifying experience and could not think of those days except with pain. Her later strong attachment to her children and unwillingness to be separated from them was rooted in those events.

Throughout life Mother maintained a childlike trust in God and a deep affection for her children. Despite only three years of schooling, she had an innate wisdom and uncanny ability of saying the right thing at the right time. She generated instant rapport with people who suffered physical pain or psychological anguish. She advised many teenagers in their tragedies, counseled young women with marriage difficulties, and in her final years shared many recollections with elderly Jewish neighbors. They all respected her highly.

Polish sayings, usually rhymed and easy to remember, rose naturally to her lips. They were so typical of her. These sayings, with their commonsense wisdom, have stayed with her children and still come to mind whenever today they face comparable situations.

Rising in the morning, I recall her saying, "Whoever rises early, on him God bestows much."[3] Perhaps that's why I've been an early riser all my life.

When we appeared to be nosey and interfering with others, she would say in Polish, "Don't stick your nose into someone else's business."[4] When there were arguments in the kitchen about what to cook for supper, she would say, "Where there are six cooks, there's nothing to eat."[5] When we spoke frivolously, she would say, "You recognize well from their speech what's going on in their head."[6]

Growing up, we possessed very little. Our household of eight experienced few luxuries. As children are accustomed to do, we occasionally expressed a desire for something our family could not afford, or we would show envy over what others possessed. Then would we hear, "Better your own hut than another's palace."[7]

She also had a saying for many months of the year. At the sight of

---

3 *Kto ranno wstaje, temu Pan Bóg daje.*

4 *Nie wścibiaj nosa do cudzego grosza.*

5 *Gdzie kucharek sześć, tam nie ma co jeść.*

6 *Znać dobrze po mowie, co się dzieje w głowie.*

7 *Lepiej swoja chatka, niż cudze pałace.*

inclement weather in April, for example, she would invariably say, "April is plaited—a bit of winter, a bit of summer."[8] A month earlier we heard, "March is like sweltering in a pot."[9]

Respect for parents was a sacred responsibility. Hence, we often heard, "Who does not listen to Mother and Father listens to the evil spirit."[10] and "God loathes such as are ashamed of their own father or mother."[11] Needless to say, we developed a deep love and affection for both parents.

The same is true of welcoming guests into the home. Mother would often say, "A guest in the home is God in the home."[12] Every person entering the house was to be treated kindly and respectfully.

Through Mother I learned to appreciate my Polish heritage and gained knowledge of many details of my ancestry on both sides. She was the inspiration for my later journeys.

---

8   *Kwiecień, plecień, wciąż preplata--troche zima, troche lata.*

9   *W marcu jak w garncu.*

10   *Kto ojca, matki nie słucha, słucha złego ducha.*

11   *Bóg sie takim brzydzi kto ojca, matka wstydzi.*

12   *Gość w dom, Bóg w dom.*

V

THE PADYKULAS

In subsequent trips to Poland and through further explorations in America, I pieced together stories about my mother's family. What in the past had been only names suddenly came to life for me. The tales were gruesome.

Anthony, Mother's one older half brother, followed her to America, but died not long afterward in a tuberculosis ward in Flemington, New Jersey, while still in his twenties. Sophie (Zosia), her orthopedically impaired younger sister whom she loved and cared for as a child in Poland, died not long after Mother's departure for America. It seems she suffered from juvenile arthritis. Mother was particularly fond of Sophie, having cared for her so tenderly.

Her sister Bertha and brother Karol, closest after her in age, suffered untold indignities during the war, both they and their families, but escaped its extreme ravages. While all her siblings experienced pain and deprivation, some faced more cruel fates than others. Among them I discovered horrid tales only hinted at in the past.

Uncle Joseph

Mother's older brother Joseph had been, from her early years, her closest companion. As a young girl she would bring lunch to him in the neighboring village where he underwent training. She departed from Poland in 1910 at age thirteen, never to see him again.

At the end of World War I, Joseph served in Marshal Piłsudski's (Peew-SOODS-key) army, which succeeded in evicting the Russians from Polish soil but not before the latter burned my mother's village to the ground. In the aftermath of the war, Poland regained its independence, and the foreign powers—Russia, Prussia and Austria—withdrew. Prussian families fled their homes in the Pomeranian region rather than live under Polish rule. Piłsudski, who played a prominent role in the new government, decreed that soldiers who assisted in the liberation of Poland would be permitted to purchase the abandoned Prussian properties. Mother's brother Joseph, therefore, took advantage of that offer and settled down as a farmer in a village near Toruń. He also encouraged his father and other relatives to abandon their burned out homes and resettle in the Pomeranian region. The land there proved more fertile and could provide a more prosperous life for them.

Hitler, however, would not forget. When the Nazis invaded in September 1939, they immediately rounded up the principal leaders of that village who occupied former Prussian-held homes and led them out to a forest clearing. All were summarily executed and buried. Uncle Joseph was then forty-four years old, and his wife was expecting their seventh child. I visited the woods and the clearing where the Nazis performed their dastardly deeds. Simple wooden crosses doted the landscape. Among them I found the name Józef Padykuła and knelt in reverence. The place is ominously called Barbarka.

AUNT VERONICA

Mother and her younger sister, Veronica, bore a striking resemblance, though the experience of the wars bore more heavily on the latter. It is said that Aunt Veronica's hair turned gray overnight as a result of a harrowing experience. During the Nazi occupation she went to town one day with her six-year-old son, Wacek, to purchase food. As they drew near to the marketplace she suddenly panicked. Searching desperately through her purse and clothing, she realized that she had forgotten to bring along her identification papers. The Nazi guard now stood only a few feet away. There was no escape. Quickly she instructed her little son to scamper home, grab the papers, and race back as fast as he could.

When the guard approached, predictably he demanded the papers. Acknowledging her forgetfulness, she begged him to please allow her to go home to pick them up. He refused. With his rifle butt he then began pushing her relentlessly toward the waiting train.

She cried and screamed. "My infant children need me at home. Please have pity," she pleaded.

"Gute mutter," he growled, "you will make a good caretaker for our noble German youth." And he continued pushing her in the direction of the train.

She dragged her feet and sought to delay, but every move of hers was met with resistance. The guard kept lifting her up and shoving her with his rifle in the direction of the boxcar. Only a few feet separated her from a frightening fate when her son came racing down the street breathless and waving the papers in his hand. Hurriedly she took the papers from his hands and presented them to the guard, who eyed them carefully and then reluctantly released her.

All the way home, amid sighs and tears, she hugged and caressed her son dearly.

UNCLE THOMAS

Among all our relatives, as far as I can determine, Uncle Thomas was the only dedicated Communist. Mother always seemed a bit embarrassed to acknowledge this. But the facts are that her younger brother's experiences of dire poverty and suffering during the Nazi period gave way to prosperity and success in the Communist era. Honestly, I have to wonder what decisions I would have made under similar circumstances.

Barely thirty when the Nazi invasion occurred, he spent several years in forced labor camps, ill-fed, poorly clothed, brutally mistreated. Unlike his older brother Joseph, Thomas did survive—but barely so.

Bad as his lot was, the fate of the Russian prisoners seemed even worse. In one of those camps, Uncle Thomas met the woman who won his heart. Much younger than he, this short, jovial, and friendly girl from Moldavia, Helena Kupców, had lost everything—family, security, and possessions. Uncle Thomas was moved by her abject poverty and charm as she sang, played the balalaika, and exuded warmth and joy. She, on the other hand, was impressed by his cleanliness, his uprightness, and his solicitude. They found comfort in each other. When the Russian troops "liberated" Poland, they married, secured employment, and began to prosper in the new Russian-controlled climate.

When communes arose, they joined them. Both labored intensely to establish a decent living for themselves and for their growing family. No other option remained for them. Uncle's industriousness resulted in his appointment as overseer of the large commune. This provided sufficient food and comfortable quarters for his enlarged family and a respectable position in the community.

Little wonder that Uncle Thomas looked with skepticism on the capitalistic system. He had all he needed and concluded that any person who worked hard under Communism could be as successful as he. Many were just too lazy, he would contend. This reminded me of the frequent discussions I had with my brother about injustice toward the poor in America. Tom, a successful tool and die maker who worked hard all his life, would respond with almost identical words, saying that a lot of people are just lazy and unwilling to work and for that reason they remain poor. One Thomas made his comments in the context of a Communist system; the other Thomas in the context of a capitalist system. Each, by the grace of God, had achieved success in their respective worlds.

At the time I met Uncle Thomas he was already in his eighties. We embraced heartily with tears of joy—he, a sprightly octogenarian steeped in Communism, and we, a younger generation of convinced capitalists. Neither of us really gave thought to ideologies or nationalities. Despite diverse life experiences, we were family, possessed of the same values and aspirations. He was a very good man whom we have grown to love and respect. And his children have become warm friends.

UNCLE ANDY

Of all my mother's kin, the one we knew best and admired most was Uncle Andy. Born the year after Mother left Poland, he did not meet her until well after World War II ended when, after years of separation in Scotland, he finally crossed the ocean and joined us in America.

At the time of the German invasion in 1939, Uncle Andy was twenty-six years old. He alone in the family escaped the joint Russian-German rape of his homeland and joined the Polish Army-in-Exile. For several years he fought under General Maciek. When the army disbanded, he could not bring himself to return to his now Russian-dominated and Communist-controlled land. He therefore settled in Aberdeen, Scotland, working for several years as a body / fender repairman. Later he came to America and gravitated between Chicago and New Jersey.

Like so many eastern European men, Uncle Andy drank and smoked heavily. He fancied himself a ladies' man, though never enough to commit to marriage. Maurice Chevalier was his favorite actor and role model. His automotive skills would enable him to secure jobs easily wherever he went, whether in Aberdeen, Scotland; Chicago, Illinois; or Trenton, New Jersey. But his early experiences predestined him to be a roamer.

At age sixty-five and in weakened health, he was taken to St. Francis Hospital in Trenton. The orderlies tied him down to protect him from himself, for in a hallucinatory rage he feared the Nazis were coming after him, as they did his younger brother, Michael. In one final flight to freedom he broke the leather straps, which bound him, and flung himself through an open window to his death several stories below. He sought escape—a tragic end to a tortured life. He had witnessed the sufferings of his brothers and sisters; he saw firsthand the savagery against his countrymen; he felt deeply the plight of Poles in Poland. Fittingly, he was buried in the Polish-American Cemetery at the Shrine of Our Lady of Częstochowa in Doylestown, Pennsylvania.

Some Polish army songs depict the Polish soldier as one wandering forever around the world, unable to find a lasting home. That was Uncle Andy. I can still hear the tender song, which his comrades, all veterans of the wars, sang at his burial in the graveyard in Pennsylvania:

"Sleep, o colleague, in this dark tomb.

May Poland appear in your dreams."[13]

UNCLE MICHAEL

Mother's brother Michael was the youngest of her nine siblings. He and Andrew were born after she departed for America. The two brothers grew up together and as young men in their twenties faced the fiendish Nazi onslaught. Andrew was fortunate to have escaped with the Polish

---

13   *Śpij, kolego, w zimnym grobie. Niechaj Polska przyśni tobie.*

Army, making his way to Italy then mustering out in England. He settled in Scotland, where he worked for many years as a body-fender man before moving to America.

Uncle Michael, on the other hand, stayed behind in Poland to deal with the satanic horde. He joined the underground and undertook secretive actions in support of his people. I know not the details of his activities during the war. The Nazis labeled him a terrorist. Only later would I learn the horrible details about his final days as described to me by my cousin. More about that later.

VI

MY FIRST VISIT TO POLAND

In the decades that followed Dad's death in 1950, I increasingly felt the need to explore my Polish roots. Older relatives had departed, and their stories were riveted in my mind. They impelled me to seek out and explore my ancestral homes.

The villages of my ancestors became my Holy Grail. I had to find them. But Poland in the fifties, sixties, and seventies did not lend itself to romantic wanderings. A gruesome environment of repression persisted long after Nazis were routed and Soviets had "liberated" its people. The Iron Curtain fell mightily on those lands, leaving the people in darkness, their hopes shattered, but their faith strong.

As years passed, the plight of Poland became more desperate and my mission more remote. Oppression grew. The Russian-imposed Communist government in Poland thwarted every attempt at self-determination, suppressing each successive revolt with impunity. And yet the uprisings continued. The Polish people would not lie still.

Beginning in the eighties, protests grew in intensity, though repression predictably followed. Polish authorities feared Soviet reprisals as had already taken place in Czechoslovakia. But the people persisted. A silent revolution began to unfold. I sensed a new world opening up, reviving old dreams and creating new possibilities. Wałęsa had not yet stormed the ramparts, but the Solidarity Movement was increasing in boldness. I resolved to go there to see for myself.

A conference in Vienna in the spring of 1989, organized by the American Gas Association on whose board I served, provided the opportunity. My employer at the time, the American Bankers Association, agreed to my attending this international business seminar in order to become better acquainted with economic conditions in that part of the world. The prospect of participating in a business meeting in the historic Austrian capital was appealing enough, but added to that was the possibility of a further flight to Warsaw to pursue my personal quest. The venture proved impossible to resist. The die was cast.

Mother had returned to Poland only once, with my sister Irene in 1962, at the height of Communist repression. More than five decades after emigrating as a teenager, she was at last reunited with her surviving brothers and sisters. Other than that visit, no other direct contact was made with our Polish relatives. When the opportunity arose for me to visit in 1989, therefore, I shared the good news with Mother. Though frail and dying, she perceived this as an unprecedented opportunity for me to meet with her family in Poland. She urged me to invite my brother Tom to accompany me on the journey. I did and he agreed. Mother unfortunately died before we embarked on our journey.

Although twelve years older than I, Tom had never visited Poland. He served with General Claire L. Chennault's Flying Tigers during World War II and preferred to tour the vast regions of our own country rather than travel abroad. Now retired from heading the Tool Room at the General Motors' Fisher Body Plant in Trenton, he had the leisure and the resources to indulge in this adventure. He shared my enthusiasm about visiting our ancestral homeland for the first time.

As we flew to Vienna, images of the past raced through my mind like the fast-forward of a sound film. I recalled the wars, the Hapsburgs, Viennese music, and more. One image that stayed with me was that of a peasant girl in a schoolhouse in Austrian-ruled Poland eighty years earlier—my mother. She attended classes for only two or three years but retained fond memories of those experiences. Each day at school began with singing the mandatory daily tribute to Emperor Franz Joseph. A revered figure, he appeared to them—regal, caring, and paternal. Well into her nineties, she would entertain us with that same song from her youth.

We traveled on the newly established Austrian Airlines. Succulent food, rich red wine, and the music of Richard Strauss made our flight an enchanting experience. Alighting in Vienna, we succumbed to its charm. We toured the museums, viewed the ornate palaces, and savored the evening entertainment. The sounds, the sights, even the smells enchanted me.

The royal splendor of the city of the Hapsburgs evoked for me other memories at the turn of the century. Those imperial palaces with their luxurious rooms and rich decorations, their princes and court attendants, presided over by the emperor contrasted starkly with my image of the Polish countryside with its lowly huts and barns, its peasant farmers and playful children. Among them frolicked my mother. Moniuszko's magnificent opera, Halka, tells of a peasant girl courted by a rich nobleman who, after a warm love affair, abandoned her for a noblewoman. The story is similar to Puccini's Madame Butterfly. Halka, the peasant, lamented her fate in an impassioned and heartwarming aria.

Vienna reminded me of Halka, of Mother, and of Poland. They each had experienced the same abandonment—Halka at the hands of a nobleman who ravished then rejected her; Mother at the hands of her family who loved her, yet sent her alone at age thirteen into a strange new land; and Poland at the hands of her neighbors who raped, and plundered and abused her for two centuries. Each faced a similar fate.

I wandered through the streets of Vienna at every opportunity. Though seemingly ancient in its buildings and monuments, it had the freshness and flavor of youth. I thrilled to its people, its restaurants, and its musical allure. All were enchanting and incomparable.

The task at hand for me, however, was an international conference. I therefore sat in on some sessions, made a presentation at another, and participated in formal gatherings to the best of my ability. The three-day conference interwove speeches, discussions, and elegant dining amid the grandeur that is Vienna. Each business session highlighted new issues of trade and banking in eastern Europe. Stimulating exchanges focused on the potential for growth and expansion in that part of the world. It was a highly successful conference.

Participants were enthralled by new opportunities for investment, but I was obsessed with only one thing—that ancestral village. When the conference ended, my brother and I, together with my brother-in-law, John Sullivan and his wife Madeline who both attended the Vienna Conference, escaped to the airport and boarded a plane for Poland. Our broader adventure was about to begin.

The flight was brief. Our Pan Am airliner descended onto the runway of the Warsaw airport and years of fantasizing and dreaming gave way to the reality of 1989. My mind was caught in a whirlwind. Would the ancestral tales prove to be mere legends? Would the region be as beautiful as they said? Are the people as noble as I had been told? In eager anticipation we awaited the unknown.

As Tom and I landed, a radiant sun beamed down on bleak surroundings—a runway patched with recent repairs and decrepit buildings decked in socialist gray. Inside the terminal we found harried travelers lined up before every counter and viewed bureaucratic bungling elevated to an art form. This was the legacy of Communism.

My first instinct was to sink to my knees and perform a John Paul II. I wanted to kiss the ground—that precious soil so drenched in human blood, that land on which my ancestors had labored for centuries, that country to which I owed so much. But I restrained myself.

The airport terminal mirrored its citizens' plight—bland, musty, and decaying. Polish officials mimicked faceless bureaucrats worldwide—cold, officious, just doing their job. And there remained the ubiquitous paperwork to be filled out, reviewed, signed and stamped, and stamped again. Such was the price we paid to enter those lands. We were willing to endure more, if only to be in Poland.

The road from the airport to the city resembled barren country roads in America—no stores along the way, no billboards, no signs, only an occasional motto on factories encouraging the citizenry to work. It reminded me of the cynical German sign at the entrance to the Auschwitz crematoria, "Work Makes One Free." The taxi driver played his stereotypical role—blaring the radio full blast, conquering corners on two wheels, threatening every moving object on the roadway. The auto, devoid of luxuries, was inappropriately called a Polonez.

Touring the city, we viewed the spectacle of nothing but ashen gray, decaying buildings—a drabness I was to see repeated throughout Poland and the entire eastern Europe. Communism clearly left poverty and uniformity in its wake. Occasional flowers on windowsills punctured the monotony, adding color to nondescript edifices. But drabness prevailed.

Our hotel, the Victoria Intercontinental, reminded me of Bogart films of my youth, where intrigue and treachery loomed at every turn. This European relic had all the elegant charm of a bygone era. A concierge with studied grace greeted us in the foyer, while sounds of many languages echoed in the background. I was particularly enchanted by the hotel doorman. A large young man with broad shoulders and handlebar mustache, he struck me as a youthful replica of my grandfather. The resemblance was uncanny. I stood back and observed the man from a distance on several occasions. Dziadek's ghost haunted me.

We wandered around Warsaw aware that this capital had been obliterated by Nazis, who boasted that it would never again arise. But here it stood. What we saw was not a newly designed city, but one painstakingly rebuilt stone by stone to resemble the original.

Warsaw in 1989 would strike any westerner as stark—no modern skyscrapers, no manicured lawns or paved superhighways, no Sears or Hyatts or McDonald's—only old buildings faced us, some well-kept and freshly painted, especially in the central city, but others decaying and in poor shape, particularly in the outer regions. Like the Man of La Mancha, I saw things differently. Faced with drab structures and desolate streets, I entertained images of Poland's noble past—its princes and artists, its palaces and sanctuaries. With quixotic vision, I toured the region, viewing the decaying Hotel Bristol and imagining grand celebrations, inhaling rancid odors from the gutters yet perceiving the fragrance of flowers, listening to the cacophony on radio, and musing about Chopin's polonaises. An inner sense transformed me.

To judge Poland only by externals would be unfair. So much pulsated within. Here lay a country raped repeatedly by its neighbors from east and west, a terrain bloodied time and again by conquering hordes, a peaceful and freedom-loving people inhumanly maltreated. Yet they persevered with unfaltering fidelity to their religious traditions.

In journeying around Warsaw, I noted graffiti on the walls of the underground passageways. Emblazoned in bold letters were the words "Czołgi do Volgi" (CHOL-gee doh VOHL-gee) meaning "Tanks to the Volga." It expressed the conviction of every Pole that Russian tanks should withdraw back to the Volga River. On visiting several years later, I noticed the same inscription unmarred, long after the offending tanks were removed. Similarly the "Arbeiten Machen Frei" (Work Makes One Free) sign was retained at Auschwitz. Poles retain for history the memories of their past, however horrid.

With reverence I lingered over the remains of the Warsaw Ghetto. A mound and marker bore witness to monumental atrocities perpetrated there. The very air cried out. I recalled the moment years earlier when, while driving with my mother and brother through Brooklyn, we had lost our way to Idlewild Airport. Suddenly we came upon a group of Hasidic Jews with black suits, large hats, and hair curled down the sides. My mother was stunned. She had not seen such a scene since leaving her small village in Poland fifty years earlier. It brought back to her fond childhood memories.

At the mound in the heart of the Warsaw Ghetto we paused. There I learned of the legendary Mordecai Anieliewicz and thousands of Jewish victims who were banded together, starved, and slaughtered. The plight of those brave Jewish defenders gripped me. In the early months of 1943, Nazi troops began the final deportation of Jews from the Warsaw Ghetto to Nazi extermination camps. Anieliewicz led the final defense against incredible odds and diabolical force. Standing in the open air, I recalled that, as that final annihilation was taking place, I myself—eight years old and totally oblivious to those events—was preparing in Trenton, New Jersey, for my First Holy Communion! The memory of those contrasting images moved me deeply.

As if the holocaust perpetrated on Polish soil was not enough, Warsaw gave further evidence of foreign barbarity. The Old Market Square, obliterated by Nazi bombs, now stands renewed. That restoration is a source of Polish pride. Pictures depicting the rubble of the city at war's end as viewed by General Eisenhower were hawked in the town square.

Along the river, tour guides pointed out the area where the Russian army waited in 1945, refusing to come to the rescue of Warsaw freedom fighters until the Nazis had eradicated all signs of life. Every Pole knows that story by heart.

The thirst for freedom remained. On the entranceway to the university, a student banner proclaimed "Free Havel." I had never before heard that name. I was told that he was a Czech author whose writings stirred and inspired the youth of these regions. Clearly solidarity among freedom seekers burned no less intense now than in the days of Pułaski and Kościuszko. And religious fervor glowed everywhere. The many churches throughout the city were not only filled to overflowing every Sunday but also crowded on weekdays—and not simply with tourists but also with local worshipers, including many youth.

In Warsaw we finally met my mother's relatives—warm, cheerful, and friendly people who arrived from several villages. There was cousin Wacek (VAH-tsek) and his ever-joyous wife Bożena (Bo-ZHEN-na), their cerebral palsied son Peter, and their charming daughter Barbara with her son Bart. Along with them came cousin Józef and his wife Janina, both schoolteachers. We cherished our common family bond.

Although a first acquaintance for each, we enkindled an immediate friendship. Decades of turmoil and devastation had separated our families, but now it was over. Long did we reminisce about the war, the historic monuments, and the whereabouts of friends and relatives. How could we compensate for two generations of brutal repression? We could try. And so we talked and explained and sought to interpret each other's experiences.

How humbling to realize that as I was growing up in a privileged environment with friendly neighbors and a good education in a free society, my cousins across the ocean were experiencing lifelong repression under party bureaucrats given to authoritarian control and rigorous indoctrination. But despite their long travail, my cousins maintained a wholesome and happy disposition. To be sure, two generations under Communism preceded by years of Nazi fiendishness had impoverished them. Yet they survived.

My initial glimpse of Poland met my expectations. Despite bleak surroundings, seedlings of renewal lay just under the surface and were about to break through. Before the end of that year, 1989, a sea storm of change would sweep in, changing not only Poland but also every nation around it. Echoes of a heroic past mingled for me with the promise of a brighter future. The nightmare for the Polish people was about to end.

VII

THE KOWALSKI
ANCESTRAL VILLAGE

My knowledge of Poland had served me well in my initial wanderings around Warsaw, but finding a small and remote village in another part of the country exceeded my talents. And that, after all, was the prime motive for my journey. When I mentioned this to cousin Wacek, he said, "No problem. I'm sure we can find it." As a taxicab driver he had traveled around the country many times and assured me he could find any place I named. Out of my wallet came the crumpled business card with the name "Antonin."

After poring over his maps for some time, Wacek was puzzled. Several villages in Poland bore that name. When I mentioned the Poznan region and the names of nearby towns identified by my aunt—Jarocin (Ya-ROH-cheen), Pyzdry (PIZZ-drie), Środa (SHRO-da)—he immediately understood. Pondering his maps, he reiterated, "We will find it. I am certain that we will find it."

According to my grandaunt, the village of my father's ancestors lay in the Poznan region, not far from the city Jarocin. Hence my relatives were referred to as Poznanians (Poznańczycy). The boundaries of that region, however, changed when the Communists took control and carved up the provinces, creating fifty-two out of seventeen units. They did this to dilute the power of the large cities. We were uncertain therefore whether the village we sought remained in the Poznan province or was now situated in one of the newly created ones. Wacek ventured that it lay on the outskirts of the newly established province of Kalisz (KAH-leesh), on the border of the province of Poznan, of which it was once a part. We set out the next day.

The journey wove through many villages adorned with roadside shrines. As we wandered around, I visualized paternal ancestors traversing the region on foot. Occasional horse-drawn carts along the roadway evoked images of simpler times and a hardier way of life. Potatoes in the field called to mind my mother's term for them—ziemniaki (zhem-NYA-key). This was the more native Polish word used in Galicja, the former Austrian sector of Poland where Mother grew up. In contrast, my father, with roots in this region, called them kartofle (kar-TOFF-leh) from the German. The language and architecture of this area clearly reflected the Prussian influence.

Wacek had driven taxis for many years. Besides having a warm sense of humor that made traveling with him very entertaining, he undertook his driving responsibilities with a religious dedication. His wife, Bożena, affirmed, "My Wacek is a very careful driver. In all his years of driving, not even a minor scratch could be found on any of his cars. And he never takes so much as a sip of wine on any day that he travels." Polish penalties for drunken driving, I came to learn, were much more severe than in our own country.

At last we arrived at large farmlands in western Poland, near what we perceived to be our long-sought village. After driving a few more miles, we spotted a small sign on the roadway with the word "Antonin."

Tom jumped out of the car and insisted that our cousin Wacek take a picture of the two of us before that sign so that we could demonstrate to our family that we had indeed found the village. It was a joyous moment for both of us.

The author, Anthony P. Kowalski, and his brother Thomas at the roadsign to the Kowalski ancestral village, Antonin.

As we drew closer, we observed a burly farmer working in the fields. I told Wacek to stop the car immediately. Then leaving the vehicle I ran up to talk with the man. After the normal pleasantries I inquired, "Are there any Kowalskis in this region?" He smiled and said, "Wait." Turning aside, he bellowed to his friend a hundred feet away, "Andrew, come over here! One of your relatives has arrived!"

The man introduced himself as Andrzej Andrzejewski (or equivalently Andrew Anderson). He listened intently to my tale about the Kowalskis from America seeking to find some long lost relatives and possibly our ancestral home. Warmly and eagerly he responded. Not he, but his mother-in-law, was the Kowalski. The village that we sought, he assured me, lay up the road a short distance. He pointed to the house where his mother-in-law lived and urged us to go there, promising to join us when he completed his labors.

Back in the car, we drove up the solitary road. Single dwellings with stone or wooden siding stood intermittently in no particular order along the flat and lush terrain. With our dress clothes we fit into the landscape like plumbers at an art gallery. No more than thirty families now lived in the village. The road was barely paved. We made our way, and the children eyed us eerily like aliens from another planet.

At the designated house I knocked on the door. A middle-aged woman appeared. Tall and broad shouldered, she resembled my aunts in New Jersey.

"Excuse me, please," I said in Polish. "My name is Antoni Kowalski. I believe that my grandfather came from this village a century ago." The woman's face lit up as I spoke. "A man up there in the fields suggested that someone here could help me."

Smiling knowingly, she said, "Please, wait here a minute." I waited patiently at the entranceway as Wacek and Tom remained in the car. I shrugged my shoulders and arms to them, signaling that I did not know what to expect. We had to be patient.

Soon the middle-aged woman returned, accompanied by a frail elderly woman in her seventies. "This is my mother, and she is by birth a Kowalski," she said.

I narrated once again the same story about my grandfather, John, and his siblings who migrated to America—Joseph, Valentine, Frances and

Mary; about their fortunes in New Jersey; and about what little I knew of their families.

After observing me intently for some time, she began her tale. I hovered over every word. Her father, Martin, remained in Poland while his brothers and sisters, including my grandfather, departed for America. This very building, she said, was the family home they left behind! Her daughter could hardly contain herself. "I recognized you as a Kowalski the moment I spotted you in the doorway," she said.

Relatives quickly gathered from the village, each recounting stories from the past. One elderly female cousin pointed to a picture on the wall depicting a wedding celebration, which had taken place almost fifty years earlier. Blushingly she acknowledged that she was that young bride. The veil she wore had been sent by a female cousin in New Jersey after her wedding. I vaguely recalled hearing as a boy that one of our cousins in South Amboy had forwarded such a garment to another cousin in Poland. And here she was!

Later I sought out the local church. In my many years working in the Catholic community, I had come to recognize the deep piety and religious fervor of the Polish people. Their family life, I realized, centered on their parish. The local church, I knew, would be the depository of records going back many years. In the late afternoon, therefore, we drove with Andrew to the neighboring village of Pogorzelica (Po-go-zhe-LEE-tsa) where we visited the parish church of St. Hyacinth. A new building had been constructed to replace the old. As we made our way past the cemetery, Andrew pointed to the grave of Marcin Kowalski, my grandfather's brother.

Fortunately the pastor was standing outside the church. Andrew introduced me, and we made small talk about America and my family and his church. After narrating my story again, I inquired about the baptismal registry for the year 1865. That year, I told the priest, was posted on my grandfather's tombstone in Trenton.

"Many of our records were destroyed during the war," he said, "but we do have some."

"Would it be possible to see them? We've traveled a long distance to be here and would like very much to verify the information."

The pastor was initially disinclined to search through the registries. "I really don't have much time. We have church services this evening, and I must begin preparations for that," he said.

"But it would mean so much to me and my family," I pleaded. "I will be happy to repay you for your efforts."

After a brief pause he said, "Well, all right. But we must do it quickly."

We entered the rectory and he departed into another room. Five minutes later he returned with the baptismal registry for 1865. Then, beginning on page one, he ceremoniously recited one name after another, fingering the handwritten entries one by one. Having had much experience in searching through baptismal and burial records in Polish script, I was tempted to grab the book and zip through the pages rapidly, but realized that deference must be shown and local practice must prevail. I was a guest and, therefore, I played the role of a patient and appreciative observer.

After an endlessly slow, page-by-page, line-by-line proclamation, we arrived at September. An entry dated September 3 listed the birth and baptism of Jan Kowalski, son of Jan and Józefa Kowalska, of the village of Antonin. I jumped up in delight.

"I can prepare a baptismal certificate for you if you like," he said.

"That would be wonderful," I responded.

He quickly copied the data, signed the document, and affixed the parish seal. We exchanged paper—he the document, I the greenbacks—and I departed a happy man.

My journey was ended. Many of my mother's family had now become my friends. And details of my father's family fit together—the village, the relatives, the bridal veil, the baptismal registry. More than forty years after my grandaunt identified the village and a full hundred years after my grandfather departed from it, I was privileged to journey back, carrying in my wallet that same business card inscribed with the village name.

Although this quest was complete, the dream endures. Forever will I cherish these people, these stories, these images. Most sacred to me, moreover, shall always be that village once mythical, now real—Antonin.

VIII

EXPLORING POLISH BANKING

The scene in Poland was rapidly changing. The curtain at last was being removed after decades of desolation, and a new nation was emerging. The triumph of the Solidarity Movement was resulting in a transformed political scene.

While serving as education director for the American Bankers Association in the fall of 1989, I was invited to a meeting in Washington arranged quickly by senior officials at the U.S. State Department who sought to respond to escalating developments in central Europe. Never before had a nation turned away from Communism. The book had not been written on how to accomplish that. Our government leaders, therefore, were eager to rush to Poland's aid and assure a successful transition, so that other nations could follow. They asked for our support.

"We have to help them," a senior official urged, "because I'm convinced this will have a domino effect. After Poland will come Czechoslovakia, then Hungary, the Baltic States, and—hold your hats—even Russia itself." A howl went up and we all had a big laugh. It seemed totally beyond the realm of possibility after decades of Cold War politics. And yet in a short time that is precisely what happened, far beyond our wildest dreams.

A new opportunity arose for me in 1990, after the overthrow of Communism. Warren Wiggins, a former Peace Corps administrator and later head of the New Transcentury Foundation, secured a grant from the German Marshall Fund to explore banking needs in Poland and develop a plan for widespread intervention in banking expansion and development with a focus on private banking. He invited me to join the team assembled for that purpose. I eagerly accepted. Caught up in the euphoria sweeping through central Europe, we set out from Dulles Airport in a large Pan Am jumbo jet.

On our first morning in Poznan, Warren and I hurried to a meeting on the other side of town. A number of people were scampering to work, and a few automobiles plied the roadway. As we traipsed along the main street in the center of town we came upon a red light at which everyone halted. No cars appeared in either direction, yet not one person dared step off the curb until the light changed. Then in unison they began walking. Years of Communist repression and legalistic demands had subjected the people to rigid conformity. Warren and I stood in amazement. After years of urban frustration trying to cross street corners in a maze of traffic in America, Warren and I could not believe what we were seeing. "Imagine that happening in Manhattan!" he remarked.

In the next two weeks we toured banks of all sizes and all types in the regions of Poznan and Warsaw. The primitive condition of banking services was reflected in stacks of handwritten and hand-stamped papers documenting every transaction. No computers in sight. Invariably a very efficient female office manager could quickly put her hands on any document we requested and explain in detail the procedures for recording every transaction. She was irreplaceable.

Our tour of banks produced some amusing stories. In one small local bank we were allowed to sit in on a meeting of the board of directors. As we entered the room, a young Solidarity leader whispered to me, "Don't take the chairman seriously. He is a Communist who ran this bank for over thirty years. But don't worry, he's really not in charge now. We tolerate him."

Sure enough, throughout the board meeting, the chairman was just a figurehead. He functioned simply as an observer who signaled the start and end of the meeting. Young turks on the board, who formed a majority, became very vocal. These Solidarity leaders allowed him to save face in the community and continue in that position, but with diminished influence on the course of affairs.

That experience introduced me to a peculiar quality of the Polish character. Despite years of suffering at the hands of cold and sometimes ruthless bureaucrats, Poles did not seek revenge on their tormentors. They arranged no showcase trials, no retaliatory measures, not even embarrassment for former overlords. A new day had dawned, and they looked to the future, not the past.

One other event in those two weeks enchanted me. Bohdan Gruchman, then Professor of Economics at the Academy in Poznan, a delightfully charming and cultured gentleman, served as our local consultant and guide. After several days of earnest investigation, Gruchman arranged a brief diversion by taking us to a surprise location. Without telling us beforehand, he drove us to a lake and we boarded an old rickety raft to a nearby island. Once there we trudged several yards along a dirt path and came upon ancient ruins. I was enthralled to discover that I was gazing on the excavated walls of the oldest royal castle in Poland, one thousand years old. Here Mieszko, the first ruler, and his son Bolesław the Brave, the first crowned king, had resided. The latter was born within those very walls.

Bohdan explained that in the tenth century the emperor of the

Holy Roman Empire visited Bolesław at this site. After leaving the island castle, they leisurely walked together to nearby Gniezno several kilometers away while servants rapidly placed red carpets before them lest the dignitaries besmirch their royal feet. That imagery and pageantry captured my imagination and hearkened me back to Poland's glorious, royal past.

After visits to many banks and discussions with many bankers, our investigating team concluded that large-scale interventions were needed. We recommended transporting senior managers for brief periods to study bank operations in the United States, bringing experts in various banking specialties as consultants to Poland, establishing train-the-trainer activities for greater long-term local impact and introducing computerization of operations on a massive scale. Many of these strategies were subsequently implemented not only in Poland but also in the entire region of Central and eastern Europe.

IX

FAMILY REVELATIONS

I wanted to share all these experiences with my wife, Joan Sullivan, and my son, John. And so in 1991, I made my third journey to Poland with them and my brother Tom. John was then thirteen years of age, the same as his grandmother when she had traveled in the opposite direction. The four of us took a guided tour of the great cities and sites of Poland. It enabled me to view for the first time and learn about places like Malbork, Zakopane (Za-ko-PA-ne), Wieliczka (Vye-LEECH-ka), and Częstochowa (Chen-sto-HO-va), while introducing Joan and John to Poznan, Cracow, and Warsaw. Guided tours in the major cities expanded my awareness and appreciation of each of those places. We also met with relatives living in Ciechocinek (Che-ho-CHEE-nek) and others who came down from Koszalin (Ko-SHA-leen).

The Baltic region, with its coastal cities of Gdynia, Gdansk, and Sopot, held a special allure for us. My wife and son both love to swim, so the proximity to the great sea made them particularly appealing. They also managed to go swimming in an indoor pool there.

In Gdansk, we saw the shipyard where Wałęsa's bold moves began and where his home is located. We viewed both. By accident, we also came upon the home of a person whose name Joan recognized. She immediately halted, insisting that I photograph her before this house so that she could show it to colleagues in the physics department at George Mason University, where she was teaching. It was the home of G. D. Fahrenheit.

Farther south we visited the famed castle of Malbork, home to the infamous Teutonic Knights. I find the very notion of a military religious order repugnant. These savage men overran Muslim villages in the Holy Land, slaying every man, woman, and child in sight. Their viciousness transcends the boundary of human decency. Their restored central fortress in Malbork is a marvel to behold, testimony to the power and ingenuity of these crafty men. Guides pointed out the trapdoor, which the grand master could easily release, tumbling their unwary guests dozens of feet to their death below. And these were religious followers of Jesus!

Not far away we were feted by a local dance group—the Kaszuby (Ka-shoo'-bi). I recall my mother telling me about them. They loved to kick up their heels and dance to native tunes, played on strange stringed instruments made of horsehairs, and showed a warmth and charm that captivated us. At one point, they whisked away Joan to the dance floor. She is always eager to dance and kept up with the best of them. Unable to speak or understand a word, she communicated joyfully through the universal language of dance. Even John, my son, was drawn into the dance by a young maiden. He too did well.

Toruń (TOE-rooyn) we visited to explore the home of Copernicus. It is now a museum. The very instruments he used were on display. My wife, a physics professor, and my son, a budding scientist, were delighted. My cousin Sophie's son, Czarek, accompanied us and took John to the pinnacle of the central church to view the entire city. Joan and I were too exhausted to climb those heights.

In Poznan, we explored farther sites unknown to me—an outdoor beehive museum, a furniture factory, and the sacred remains of the first two rulers of Poland—Mieszko and Bolesław the Brave. With others we gawked at the noonday pageant in the clock tower of the town center. And as we departed the region, the vision of my ancestors strolling these very roads captivated me. This is where they lived and toiled for many generations.

Then we traveled to southern Poland and the mountains near Zakopane (Za-ko-PA-neh), followed by the salt mines in Wieliczka (Vye-LEECH-ka) and the priceless treasures of Cracow. The latter ranks among my favorite cities. Here on Wawel (VA-vel) Hill is found the church and repository of Poland's greatest kings, artists, and scholars. Here also stood the Jagiellonian University, established in AD 1364, the magnificent paintings of Matejko (Ma-TEY-ko), the Marian Church with its legendary trumpeter who heralds each hour, and numerous theaters and museums. All proved to be a magnet for me and my family.

We toured Kazimierz, the former Jewish sector of Cracow, where Yiddish theater once thrived and Jewish scholarship flourished. Now only a cemetery and emptied buildings stood as testimony to the past. Not many miles away lay the horrific Auschwitz. As joyous as my visits to Poland have always been, a haunting counterpoint engulfs me whenever I perceive remnants of a cherished culture that deserved to endure. Muted voices stalked the air. Their echoes thunderously reverberated within my soul.

Before returning to America, we spent a few days with our relatives. In Warsaw, my cousin, Józef Modeński, met us and offered to take us on a walking tour of the city. We had toured the city on bus with a large group during our first trip. But this would be different. An educated man and teacher of handicapped children, Józef had witnessed firsthand and studied details of World War II in Poland. He was the son of my mother's sister, Veronica, and for some reason during the war had changed his last name from the revered Mickiewicz to Modeński. He now masterfully shared with us some of the more tragic details about our family.

My sister Irene had met him on her one journey with Mother in the sixties. She informed me of his accurate knowledge of many events in Poland and his delight in narrating them. For years I had yearned to learn from him. Upon my request, therefore, he took us to a series of buildings in Warsaw, which during World War II housed the German High Command. On the street in front of the building he reenacted with dramatic flair a plot of treachery and defiance.

"On that corner stood a young girl with a purse on one shoulder. She nonchalantly observed activities in the courtyard. When she saw the Commandant enter his limousine, she removed the purse from one shoulder and moved it to the other. That was the signal. Two blocks away another partisan signaled to his comrades. When the Commandant's limousine reached a designated spot, the comrade lit a cigarette. Then it happened."

Joseph had acted out that scene many times, every gesture dramatized for effect. The suspense built up as he spoke. Underground leaders had planned to kill the infamous Commandant. All were in position to execute the plan. At the appointed time, the Commandant entered his chauffeured auto. Partisans relayed the appropriate signals. When the car reached the preordained spot, the bomb exploded and achieved its objective. The Commandant was murdered. Panic and pandemonium erupted, followed by fierce reprisals. Increased terror ensued as the Gestapo determined to set an example. In an unprecedented display of savagery, they retaliated by rounding up and killing dozens of Poles. They would penalize every act of terrorism against them while perpetrating gargantuan acts of terrorism of their own. "It was a high price to pay," Joseph said, "but the underground had succeeded with their plan."

We then toured the offices of the former German Chancellery, all well kept, with flowers displayed in the windows everywhere. Little evidence of the previous bestiality and carnage remained. As we wandered into another building, Joseph began telling us the story of our Uncle Michael, my mother's youngest brother. He was twenty-five years old when the war broke out. Unlike older brother Andrew, he did not have the opportunity to escape and enlist with Polish forces in exile. He therefore joined the underground.

We do not know the precise nature of his activities though Nazis referred to him as a terrorist. Eventually the Nazis captured him. As we approached the next building Joseph said, "This is where they imprisoned him." It was a bare, solidly constructed building. I could visualize the entire scenario which he then described.

"When I was only six years old, I accompanied my mother on a visit to Uncle Michael. She entered the prison, but I was not allowed inside. I had to wait on that very corner over there." He pointed to the intersection not far away.

"We visited here several times. Mother was always distressed when she emerged. I remember the last time we arrived. The Nazi officer matter-of-factly informed her that Michał Padykuła was no longer there. She panicked, realizing what it meant. Days later his name appeared on the list of deceased regularly published by the Nazi regime."

With Joseph, we entered that prison in the former headquarters of the German High Command, now a small museum. As we approached, darkness and eerie silence greeted us. Immediately we sensed that we stood on sacred ground. Passing through the dimly lit entranceway, we came upon a wall with candles and other decorations artfully arranged. Words on the wall of the entranceway had once been inscribed in one of the cells. It read in Polish:

"'Tis easy to speak about Poland,
more difficult to work for her,
much more difficult to die for her,
but most difficult to suffer for her."

We stood in the entrance to the torture chambers of the Nazi SS guards. The first rooms functioned as interrogation centers. Clumsy chairs to which the prisoners were strapped stared at us, with fiendish instruments of torture nearby. Cousin Joseph boasted proudly, "Uncle Michael spent several weeks here, but there is no evidence that he ever gave in to his captors. He never revealed anything about the Polish underground or the whereabouts of his friends. They could never break Uncle Michael."

Down the corridor, we viewed some of the small cells—no windows, a smell of dampness, almost total darkness. Lavatory facilities were nonexistent for these short-term guests from whom the Gestapo would extract either information or life. Frequently both.

From the prison, we proceeded to a nearby wall. It served as a place of execution. The bullet-pocked wall was all that remained of that grizzly history. Uncle Michael most likely had been killed there, but we could not be sure. His remains were never found.

The sun shone beautifully as we went on to stroll through streets where Nazi chieftains once reigned. The universally drab gray buildings of the city still endure, though now adorned with flowers and decorations. They serve as government buildings of the Polish state.

Bittersweet memories remain—of man's inhumanity to man, of Polish patriotism and heroism, of the indomitable drive to freedom and survival. All engulfed me in that brief visit to the depths of hell.

X

THE PADYKULA
ANCESTRAL VILLAGE

The quest for one more village remained—my mother's. In 1995, I had the opportunity to search for her native village with my brother Tom amid circumstances similar to the discovery of our father's ancestral home. Fortune had led me to accept an assignment to work for a year in Nowy Sącz, near the border of Poland and Slovakia. I served as liaison between Polish and American groups and bore the title of dean of the new business school in the town. After several months of labor there and foreseeing a week's hiatus from my work, I phoned my brother and suggested his joining me in a new quest, this time for Mother's native village. He needed no coaxing. He flew in and another adventure began.

Mother always identified herself as a Galician (Galicjanka), a native of that portion of Central Europe which includes the southeastern section of present-day Poland. As part of the Austro-Hungarian empire, that region was ruled in the nineteenth century by the Hapsburgs.

The eldest daughter and second child of the union of John Padykula and Catherine Sypek, Mother was baptized Marianna Padykuła in Wadowice Gorne. Not to be confused with the birthplace of Pope John Paul II, this small village is located farther to the east, near the town of Mielec. In more recent days, I have scrambled through bookstores and libraries in Poland, trying to find out more about that locale, all to no avail. For me therefore its main claim to fame is my mother.

At my place of employment, the Higher School of Business (Wyższa Szkoła Biznesu) in Nowy Sącz, I secured the services of a worker, Jasiu Bochenek, who agreed to transport us. He was different than Wacek. Once behind the wheel, this mild-mannered man underwent a Clark Kent transformation. A sense of power overwhelmed him as he commandeered his Polonez with the determination of a speed car racer. From time to time, he would sit up in his seat, grab hold of the wheel, and floor the accelerator with obvious delight. We marveled at this transformation.

Along the journey from Nowy Sącz, many small villages lay before us, as well as farmlands and hills to the south. Unlike the large farms and prosperous agriculture near Poznan, this region seemed genuinely poor. It had suffered from proximity to the eastern border and from continuous warfare waged relentlessly around it. Aside from the ravages of two World Wars, the landscape could not have changed much from the time my mother departed eighty years earlier.

Eventually we spotted a sign off the main highway marked Wadowice Górne. A few kilometers up the road at an intersection with a wayside shrine on the left and a church directly before us we stopped. St. Anne's Church faced us. Mother had often mentioned her little wooden parish chapel but here stood a brick structure. Finding the front door locked, I wandered in and around the church grounds. A door in the rear was open, so I entered and found myself in the sacristy. Hearing some shuffling of feet not far away, I called out. An elderly priest who had been arranging decorations on the altar soon appeared. When I told him the story about my mother, he eagerly agreed to help.

We first strolled through the church as he narrated its history and called attention to the photos in the rear depicting wartime devastation. The current building, I learned, was constructed a few years after my mother left for America. It was again remodeled after World War II. On leaving the church, he pointed to the location of the original wooden structure, which had been transferred to another village not far away. Then he invited us into his rectory.

He answered my questions directly. The village has always remained poor, he said. Not many Padykulas in town now though the name was common in the cemetery. My grandfather, I knew, had moved his entire family northwest after World War I, so most of my relatives now resided near the city of Toruń. But like me, their roots lay here.

I requested to see the baptismal record of my mother for November 29, 1896. "Of course," he said. Immediately he departed to a nearby room to retrieve the appropriate volume. He returned shortly and in a sad tone observed, "I'm sorry." Then he showed me. The very page we sought was missing; someone had torn it out. I could not verify my mother's baptism. Disappointed, I asked to view the record for the previous year and quickly found the baptismal record of Mother's older brother, Joseph. Then paging down a few years I noted entries for my Aunt Bertha (Bronisława) and Aunt Veronica (Weronika), both next in age after my mother. The facts were clear.

I next inquired about my grandparents' wedding. The priest was willing to search further. Uncertain of the exact year, I knew that Mother was born in late 1896 and her one older brother in 1895. So we tried 1894 and struck gold. An entry recorded the marriage of Jan (John) Padykuła, then thirty-three years of age, and Katarzyna (Catherine) Sypek, then nineteen years of age. A special notation in Latin indicated that the bride's father gave permission for his daughter to marry despite her young age. It was signed by Michał Sypek, my great-grandfather. Delighted with the finding, I requested a copy of that record, which the pastor gladly prepared.

Not far from the church and across the street lay the parish cemetery. The pastor warned that I would find no gravestone dated earlier than the forties. Although many people were buried there, the bombing and devastation during the war years had destroyed all traces. I recalled Mother saying, after her only return visit, that she had sought in vain the burial site of her mother. My mother's sisters had taken her to one location and pointed to a huge crater resulting from a bomb being dropped during the war. Among the debris had been her mother's tomb. All the remains were then reburied together in one huge plot. We knew not where to find it.

Fortified by the pastor's cautions, I wandered off to the graveyard. No dates on the tombstones antedated the war, but the names inscribed were significant. Besides the Padykulas, I found the maiden names of my grandmothers, Sypek and Ogorzalek, and that of my great-grandmother, Midura. Other names I recognized from our parish in Trenton, New Jersey, where many from this region had settled—Kulig, Dziura, and Maziarz. For a long time I roamed around those grounds with thoughts of my ancestors running through my mind. The spirits of the dead seemed to speak to me.

The houses in the region and the way of life there had remained unchanged for generations. The peaceful repose of the village revealed a world far removed from the hustle and bustle of the new world in which my mother had suddenly been thrown. It was fascinating for me to observe the way of life she had left behind. What would she have been forced to endure if she had remained!

Before leaving the United States, I had secured from a cousin in

Providence, Rhode Island, the address of a distant relative in Wadowice Górne. Armed with that information, I stopped people along the road for help. Some never heard the name, Walter Sypek. One woman, however, set us in the right direction, noting that the number that accompanied the address was not a street number but a village number, No wonder we did not know how to interpret it. We then drove up the road a short distance from the cemetery.

About three kilometers away we came upon a house, saw children playing in the yard, and spied a middle-aged woman nearby. I went up to her and asked if Walter Sypek lived there. She pointed to a frail man standing in the distance with a cane in hand, observing me cautiously. I told him that I had traveled from America, that I thought we might be cousins, and that I would like to talk with him. Hesitantly, he welcomed us into his home.

The house, like so many in the region, was a plain brick building with bare essentials. We sat in the living room, and I began my story about Mother and our family and what little I knew about the Sypeks. He asked his daughter-in-law to bring in a bag filled with family photographs. Reaching in, he displayed them one by one. The first was dated around 1910—a picture which I have treasured in my own home for many years. It depicts Michał Sypek and Marya Midura Sypek, my great-grandparents. Walter claimed they were his as well. From then on, he and I quickly warmed up to each other.

Michał Sypek was my mother's beloved grandfather who would frolic with her and allow her to savor the nectar in his beehives. Villagers would flock to his home, Mother said, to read letters from abroad or help them sign documents. He was, it seems, one of the few in his community who could read and write.

My great-grandparents, Michał and
Marianna Sypek, c. 1910.

Walter then pulled out other photos, which I readily recognized. One showed my mother in 1962, on her one return visit to that village. Another, from the same journey, portrayed my sister Irene clumsily perched on a horse in that yard. Included also were photos of our relatives, the Lonczaks in Providence, and one depicting my uncle Andy with Walter's father, John Sypek, taken when the latter had visited his sister, Mary Lonczak, in America. Uncle Andy had joined him on that occasion.

Walter erroneously referred to Mother's younger brother, Andrew, as a barber (fryzjer). Uncle Andy had spent a brief period of some time in the town of Mielec in the years immediately preceding the war. I remember his rough fat hands and stubby fingers, reflecting a lifetime spent working on cars as a body-fender man. I could never picture him as a barber and found the very idea hilarious. Walter was obviously mistaken.

Only sixty-four years of age, Walter Sypek had suffered a heart attack, which had slowed him considerably. He trudged along with a cane and would not be rushed at anything. I tested his memory to determine precisely our ancestry and jotted down the details. The name Sobek (Sebastian) Sypek came up, and my brother and I smiled. Mother and Uncle Andy had mentioned his name many times. Sobek, it turns out, was my grandmother's brother. Therefore, John Sypek, Sobek's son, and Mary Lonczak, his daughter, were first cousins to my mother. That made Walter Sypek my second cousin. The mystery of our relationship was solved.

Walter then revealed that our great-grandparents' original house was situated not far from the building in which we were standing. It had long ago been torn down. In the rear of the house, his son outlined the lands, which he and many generations of Sypeks before him had plowed. I viewed those fields for a moment in meditation like Patton on the ancient battlefield.

Nearby were the beehives where Mother had played alongside her grandfather. She had a special relationship with him and would follow him around the yard during his round of chores.

A very old wagon lay in the yard. Walter urged me to stand atop it with my brother for a historic photograph. I quickly obliged. We can't be sure, but this may have been the same wagon that our great-grandfather used a century ago. It certainly looked that old. I proudly stood atop it.

Before departing, I asked him to point out the location of my grandparents' home. He did. It lay just down the road, around six houses away. Mother told us about running up often to visit with her grandparents. As we drove away, I had to pause near the current house, for many decades occupied by others, but once the abode of my mother's childhood.

Mother went on to live her own life while keeping contact by mail with some of her siblings through the years. Like them, she married and had a large family. The horrors of the war years and the subsequent Communist plague eluded her. She was glad for that. Nevertheless, she often grieved over the loss of her parents, the suffering of her siblings, and the plight of her homeland.

When she returned to Poland in 1962 after more than half a century, she was reunited with remaining siblings—brothers Karol and Thomas and sisters Bertha and Veronica. She struck them as a typical wealthy American, unburdened by the horrors of war and the poverty of the Communist system. Though far from wealthy, Mother nevertheless enjoyed in America the freedom and prosperity which they craved.

In March 1989, Mother died at the age of ninety-two. This took place two months before the joyous reunion of her two sons with her brother Thomas and his family, and six months before the liberation of her homeland from the yoke of Communism. Tragically, these experiences of joy and liberation would be denied to her. The fruit of all her prayers and yearnings over many years would be enjoyed not by her but by her children. All those remarkable events of 1989—the joyous reunion of her brother and sons, the victory of the Solidarity Movement, the liberation of her homeland, the overthrow of Communism, the fall of the Berlin Wall—all transpired before the end of the year of her death. That year therefore carries mixed signals for us, her children.

Though unable to witness those events, she died with the satisfaction of completing a marvelously rich life. The world was at peace, a Polish pope sat in Rome, and her children were happy and successful. What more could she ask of God?

XI

MY YEAR IN POLAND

After all these journeys, I was fortunate to spend one full year in Poland, thanks to an offer from National Louis University, centered in Chicago. They asked me to assist in their name with the establishment of a new business school in Poland. It was an offer I could not refuse. I was eager to assist in the remarkable transformation taking place in Poland. My year of academic service during 1994–95 enabled me to become further acquainted with the region of southeastern Poland, where I resided.

From my base in Nowy Sącz (NOH-vy Sonch), I set out on weekends to discover for myself many unique villages and historic locations. These included the mineral springs in Krynice (Kry-NYEE-tse), as well as quaint villages like Muszyna (Moo-SHYH-na), Piwniczka (Pyv-NYEECH-ka) and Rabka. There were also historic museums in Tarnów (TAR-noof), Stary Sącz (STA-ry Sonch), and Nowy Sącz; and unusual attractions like the public market in Nowy Targ (NOH-vy Targ) and the bee center in Kamianna (Ka-MYAN-na). Further explorations of the mountainous region around Zakopane also followed.

The mineral springs posed a unique attraction. In the first months of my stay that year I took the train to Krynice. I had heard of the almost miraculous quality of its water and its perceived therapeutic value for all types of ailments. In this remote area where the famed Polish tenor, Jan Kiepura, once lived, I wandered among the visitors and experienced a far different ambience.

People traveled there from all over Poland. Many were elegantly attired and took delight in strolling around the hall with their own fancy mugs containing their chosen brand of water. I tasted what was touted as the best. Ugh! The charm of the entire experience impressed me even though the water repulsed me. I could not understand how people could delight in such potions. But in my earlier years I would have concluded the same about drinking beer.

In Tarnów I viewed a number of distinctive museums and exhibits. One was a Gypsy museum portraying the entire history of those interesting but tragically persecuted people. In the town center are found religious and governmental museums containing treasures from the city's marvelous past. The paintings of distinguished local noblemen especially impressed me. In the center of town, I also found a memorial to one of its famous sons, General Bem who, I learned, became a Muslim convert. Given the overwhelming Catholic presence in Poland, I found the esteem and reverence shown this man remarkable. His monument stands in the midst of a strongly Catholic community. In an age of religious bigotry, especially toward Muslims, this statue stands as a beacon.

Not far away I also discovered an Irish pub, the only one I came upon in Poland. In honor of my wife I determined to have a pawter, but unfortunately the pub was closed. I would have liked to entertain my wife and my Irish friends at home with tales of the Irish pub in Poland.

In one of the tour books I discovered that Lenin resided in this region of Poland for several years as he eluded the Czar's troops. The book indicated that for a brief period he was imprisoned in nearby Nowy Targ

(NOE-vy Targ). During the Communist era, many devoted Leninists, I'm told, had made the journey here like Christians and Muslims on pilgrimage to their sacred shrines. They sought to retrace the route traveled by Lenin from Nowy Targ to St. Petersburg, as he returned to Mother Russia to take charge of the Russian Revolution. I was determined to find that jail.

Nowy Targ, which means new market, is famed for its huge marketplace where merchants come daily from afar to display their wares. One could hear Russian, Ukrainian, Slovak, and other foreign languages among the merchants who plied their trade. I inquired of several inhabitants about the prison in which Lenin was jailed. Most ignored me. One cab driver pointed in the general direction, so I ventured on foot. The people I met along the way didn't know what I was talking about.

Suddenly I spied two elderly gentlemen strolling falteringly along the way. When I inquired, they immediately registered awareness. "Come with us," they smilingly said. A few blocks away we came upon a dilapidated building no longer in use, the walls of which were covered with children's drawings of flowers and greenery. That was the former jail. They pointed to one small window which they claimed peered into Lenin's prison cell. I got up close to look in.

"Is there any monument or inscription that would register this historic landmark?" I asked. They laughed. "No one today wants to even admit that he was imprisoned there," they said. In departing I took photographs of what was for me a memorable moment.

On another occasion, I traveled to visit the remote town of Gorlice (Gor-LEE-tseh). There I met in a local museum with the mayor who revealed to me the important history of this region. It seems that many years earlier a historic battle was fought there in which the Poles resoundingly defeated the Russians. During the period of Communist and Russian control, it was unpopular for Poles to celebrate that historic event. And so it was ignored even in the history books. But now that the Soviet menace no longer hovered over them, Poles could attempt to publish the truth. The mayor invited me to return a month later for the anniversary celebration when the history of past glory would be proclaimed loud and clear. My schedule did not permit me to return.

One weekend I took the train to another town the tour book revealed to me, Biecz (Byech). The place had a unique charm. Queen Hedwig, lured by the picturesque countryside obvious even today, spent her vacations in a nearby castle. Famed as a halfway storage area for the well-regarded Hungarian wines, the town stored vast quantities of this precious commodity on its journey to northern markets. Only one huge keg of hundreds once stored there now remained as a monument to that era. But there were also two other museums worth visiting. The outlying region, despite its natural beauty, was heavily devastated during the wars. Poverty now engulfed the town.

A memorable site for me in Nowy Sącz was the art gallery, which had formerly housed the Jewish synagogue. It was once the central meeting place for the Jewish citizenry who, prior to the war, numbered almost a majority in the town. Here resided the saintly rabbi, Chaim Halberstam, whom Jewish faithful from far and wide would travel to for counsel. I remember seeing at the museum pictures of this diminutive figure, seemingly less than five feet tall, with the outsized influence throughout the region. He is referred to by the Polish people as a cadyk (TSA-dyk), a term designating religious leader of the Chassidim.

In the city of Nowy Sącz also lay the ruins of the palace which King Casimir the Great built and where the distinguished Polish historian Jan Długosz, tutor to the princes, wrote his memorable Historia Poloniae, the history of the Polish people. Now only rubble remained at this historic locale. The Nazis used it as the roundup area for the Jews of the town before shipping them off to Auschwitz. It also served as fortification for all their artillery. Before departing, the Nazis exploded everything in sight. Only bare ruins remain. I took pictures of the "Baszta Kowalska," the Blacksmith's Tower, one of the few remaining sections of the castle wall.

I was invited to the art gallery in Nowy Sącz on one occasion to attend an international conference organized by the college where I worked. Among the participants was a German military officer. I gulped at the prospect of a German in military uniform at this site of unimaginable German atrocities. But my fears were ungrounded. At the scheduled time he arose in full uniform, but in contrast to arrogance in the past, he spoke softly yet eloquently of the different role of the military in a modern state. His remarks were admirable and noteworthy. I could hardly believe my ears. Obviously a new era was upon us, and past horrors would have to be set aside in the interest of lasting peace.

Time changes our view of things. These experiences have led me to reconsider my perceptions of the past. The frequent allegations of anti-Semitism against Poles is one proposition that has always disturbed me. None of such bigotry did I ever experience from my parents. Yet the repetition of those allegations and the occasional bigoted remarks by clerics and political leaders even in our day in Poland provide a basis for such repeated charges. Fortunately, Pope John Paul II has contributed significantly to changing the climate of Jewish-Catholic relations.

How noble, I thought, of the Scandinavian people to don Jewish insignia in the face of Nazi aggression so as not to distinguish themselves from their neighbors. Why did not the Polish people during World War II respond similarly? When I asked him that, my good friend, Janusz Jaworski, a professor at the School of Economics in Cracow, had an answer. "You've got to understand, Tony," he said, "the degree of terror generated by the Nazis in Poland. For concealing a handgun in the home, the head of the household was taken out and publicly slain; but for concealing a Jewish child, the entire household was publicly dragged before the entire community and executed, and their house burned to the ground. In no other country were such extremes of terrorism applied."

In the same region of southern Poland I was fascinated by the older town of Stary Sącz (Old Drain). Around ten kilometers from Nowy Sącz (New Drain), it was established in the thirteenth century, only a generation or two before the latter. At the center of the town lay one of the earliest Poor Clare monasteries in the world, dating from the days of Clare herself. Famed for the memory of the Blessed Kinga, who retired to the monastery after the death of her royal husband and served as Mother Abbess for many years, this heavily cloistered monastery has been in continuous use through all these centuries. Many young girls in that region, I learned, were named Kinga.

The town of Stary Sącz is also famed for two other events. Here the great King Jan Sobieski, after his great victory over the Turks at Vienna, was reunited with his beloved wife Marysienka (Mah-ry-SHEN-ka). His passionate love letters bear witness to the romantic side of this warrior. Their mutual correspondence parallels in many ways the letters of John and Abigail Adams in America. During the course of my stay in Stary Sącz, I managed to dine at the restaurant there, appropriately named Marysienka. A monument nearby bears witness to her joyous reunion with her husband.

Here too is the birthplace of the well-known diva of the New York Metropolitan Opera in the early part of the twentieth century, Ada Sari. Born Jadwiga Schayer to a prominent Jewish family, she received her early vocal training from the Poor Clare Sisters at the monastery. Throughout her life, she retained fond memories of the region and of the sisters.

On another occasion, I toured Wrocław (VROTS-wav), the former Prussian town of Breslau, now the center of an important university and the site of a large Catholic enclave containing seminary, convents, and episcopal residence. The latter area is referred to by the inhabitants as their own Vatican. The city was once a center of Prussian culture.

On a tour of Wrocław, I came upon a café owner who prepared lunch for us. Hearing that I was an American, this portly gentleman with a philosophical bent proffered to me his solution for Poland's present disastrous dilemma. With a straight face, he declared, "Poland should immediately declare war on the United States. Then upon engaging in military maneuvers, it should just as quickly surrender. America would then be led to invest in Poland huge amounts of money just as it did in Germany and Japan after defeating them in the World War II." He reflected the widespread feeling of regret that the United States and Britain had turned Poland over to Stalin and Communism, while simultaneously investing millions through the Marshall Plan and granting full freedom and democracy to the former Nazis who had fought them bitterly. Memories of those injustices are difficult to suppress.

All these experiences gave me a deepened awareness of that which I had learned from my boyhood. The Poland of my grandparents at the turn of the previous century was a pastoral land where farmers and laborers lived under foreign control yet in relative peace. The Poland of my contemporaries in the twentieth century was a land of bloody repression, barbaric cruelty, and denial of basic freedoms. Fortunately, my parents and my siblings had bypassed all of that. Only vicariously, through the stories of relatives and friends, could I relive those horrors. Never again!

XII

KAROL WOJTYŁA,
POPE JOHN PAUL II

One of the heroes of modern Poland is Karol Wojtyła. His life embodies the experience of Poland in the twentieth century—its sorrows and tragedies, its successes and triumphs. He always identified with the Polish people. He lived through their brutal enslavement under Nazi oppressors and their denial of freedom and human rights under imposed Communist collaborators. And yet he lived to see the overthrow of both. His story is instructive for all.

After six score years of suppression, Poland became a liberated nation in 1919 with the signing of the Treaty of Versailles. Poles were once again free. This event aroused great patriotism and devotion among all its citizens. A year later, Karol Wojtyła was born in Wadowice, not far from the ancient capital of Cracow, where Polish kings and heroes lay buried on Wawel Hill. His parents were fervent Catholics and staunch patriots, dedicated to a free and independent Poland.

Wojtyła received a good basic education. His brother went on to medicine, and he, no surprise, chose to major in Polish literature.

He became active in student theater and even composed both poetry and drama. However, like Poland itself, he was forced to curtail all independent activity as a result of the German invasion in September, 1939. His leisurely pursuit of the arts ended.

Hitler considered Poles an inferior race. He therefore closed all secondary schools and universities, slaughtered countless professionals of every kind, and handed over the entire populace to sadistic German generals who ruled mercilessly. The church was forbidden to celebrate the feasts of Polish saints. A superior culture, presumably, would prevail.

Wojtyła was assigned to hard labor as a stone breaker at Solvay's Zakrzówek quarry, then later as a worker at Solvay's factory at Borek Fałęcki. He performed for a while with the Rhapsodic Theater, which was still permitted to function. But soon he felt a higher calling. In the fall of 1942, he went to the residence of Cardinal Sapieha in Cracow and requested that he be allowed to study for the priesthood. The cardinal designated a priest theologian to privately guide his studies.

The routine of work and study continued until Russians evicted the Nazi forces from Poland. The Germans, in full-scale retreat, followed a scorched earth policy. They would have leveled Cracow as they did Warsaw were it not for astute Cracovians who removed and destroyed explosives which had been placed at various strategic locations throughout the city.

When war ended, the Iron Curtain fell, and Poles were still not free. They had to live in a totalitarian state with controlled media, unfriendly to religion. Wojtyła, nevertheless, was ordained a priest and was permitted to go to Rome for further theological study. His first pastoral experience would take place in the parish of Niegowić in 1948.

After eight months, Cardinal Sapieha wisely transferred him to the university parish of St. Florian in Cracow. There he gained popularity with the young people, maintaining a warm rapport and relationship with them, which continued throughout his life. He also became a lecturer in Christian ethics at the Jagiellonian University. In 1954, when the government closed the theological faculty there, Wojtyła began teaching ethics at the Catholic University of Lublin (KUL).

Effective pastoral ministry led to his promotion as auxiliary bishop in 1958. When the archbishop of Cracow died in 1963, Communist authorities were determined to see to a replacement who would be easier to work with. They had become frustrated with the intransigence of Cardinal Wyszynski, the Primate of Poland. They therefore rejected the first three names Wyszynski proposed and the second three as well. Finally Wojtyła's name appeared on the third list, and they approved. They judged him to be seemingly reticent about politics and more interested in academic matters.

Significantly, Wojtyła's attire at his installation in the Wawel Cathedral was tied into Polish history—a chasuble from Queen Anna Jagiellon (sixteenth century), a pallium from Queen Jadwiga (sixteenth century), a mitre from the famous Bishop Andrzej Lipski (sixteenth century), a crozier from the days of King Jan Sobieski (sixteenth century), and a ring from Bishop Mauritius, fourth successor to the martyred St. Stanislaus (twelfth century). Proud patriot, he would embody in his garments the proud history of Poland through the ages.

He participated in events at the Second Vatican Council, where he played a minor role. After the council, at age 46, he was made a cardinal. This resulted in Poland having two cardinals, and some feared that it would dilute the power of the primate, Wyszynski. But that never happened. They worked well together.

In the meantime, Wojtyła's name gained greater recognition among bishops worldwide. He served on papal committees, including the Birth Control Commission. When in 1978, the See of Rome became vacant for a second time, much debate about a successor followed. Through efforts of cardinals like Franz Koenig of Vienna and John Krol of Philadelphia, Karol Wojtyła became the choice of a majority. He took the name John Paul II.

In subsequent return trips to Poland, he mesmerized the masses with his strong and uplifting message. He preached boldly before bewildered and somewhat helpless Communist officials. The rest is history. On his watch (assisted by his behind-the- scenes maneuvers), Communism was eradicated from Europe. Similarly, anti-Semitism was at last addressed as Rome finally recognized the State of Israel, and Wojtyła prayerfully visited the Holy Land. Ecumenical relations also advanced significantly.

Pope John Paul II remained a Polish patriot through and through. He strode the stage of history as few Poles ever have, and this after the barbaric subjugation and ruthless repression of him and his people. His place in the pantheon of Polish greats is assured. And yet, more must be said.

REASSESSMENT

Our perspective on history must always be tempered by additional data and further developments in time. It also helps to view events from the perspective of others. Our judgments thereby become chastened. So is it for me with Franklin Delano Roosevelt, Winston Churchill, Ronald Reagan, and Karol Wojtyła.

I grew up in a household which revered Roosevelt and felt charmed by the wit and doggedness of Churchill. My parents had survived perhaps two years of near destitution—unemployed, with no income, and dependent on the charity of others. They attributed much of their turnaround to Roosevelt and the New Deal. Dad was eager to gain employment and support his growing household of eight. When he was finally hired in the potteries, he became a lifelong supporter of the labor movement and the Democratic Party. Both parents would never again think of voting for anyone but a Democrat. To do otherwise would be to support the very plutocrats who drove the nation into recession.

I imbibed the same attitude and, when it came to dismantling the New Deal and once again favoring the rich over the poor, I opposed Ronald Reagan. My brother, on the other hand, by then comfortable in his management position at General Motors, thought otherwise.

It helps to walk in the shoes of others. I have come to recognize that the citizens of Poland think very differently about these personages. They revere Ronald Reagan and rightly so. Reagan championed the liberation of the Polish people from the yoke of Russian Communism. Poles hold in less esteem Roosevelt and Churchill, who permitted that very yoke to be placed on them at Yalta.

Roosevelt was already a sick man and acquiesced too readily to the demands of the madman Stalin. As for Churchill, he had available to him in London since 1939 offices of the Polish government–in–exile— the very voice of the Polish people. He could have sought their advice, especially in view of the long-standing treaty between Poland and Great Britain. Both he and Roosevelt ignored that voice.

My views of Wojtyła must also be reexamined in light of the plight of progressive Catholics worldwide today. True, he was instrumental in lifting the Iron Curtain and ending Communism in eastern Europe; true, he sought to breach the gap between the church and our long-suffering Jewish brothers and sisters; true also, he established better relations with people of other faiths to a degree hitherto unknown. But the inner working of the church in our day has been sadly compromised.

The litany is long—the extraordinary centralization of power; the extreme clericalization of the church; the obstinate refusal to even discuss the sacramental ministry of women; and cover-up of the sexual abuse of our children by clergy and religious, with lack of episcopal accountability.

Perhaps University of Notre Dame theologian Richard McBrien put it best when he wrote, "When the final assessment of John Paul II's long pontificate is rendered, it is likely that historians will notice the sharp contrast between the pope's major successes on the extra-ecclesial front and his equally major failures on the intra-ecclesial front." He remains nevertheless a broadly admired and respected figure.

My sister, Irene Kowalski, with Pope John Paul II in Rome, c. 2000.

MY SISTER IRENE

Around the year 2000, my beautiful sister, Irene, traveled with a group of friends on a pilgrimage to Rome. While standing in a crowd as the aging Polish pope processed along, she shouted out to him in Polish, "My mother came from Wadowice." That immediately caught his attention, as she knew it would. He stopped in his tracks and walked over to her to find out more.

Irene then confessed that her mother was born in a small village, which carried the same name as his hometown. Hers was the village of Wadowice Górne (Wadowice Hills) in the province of Mielec, northeast of Cracow; his was the town of Wadowice, slightly southwest of Cracow. They lie around a hundred miles apart.

The stratagem served Irene well. A photographer captured the moment forever on film—she holding hands with her revered Pope John Paul II, her friends nearby in witness. Our family cherishes that moment caught forever on film.

XIII

THE EAGLE

According to legend, three brothers—Lech, Czech, and Rus—went hunting one day. They each followed a different prey and traveled in diverse directions. Rus headed eastward to the plains of modern Russia; Czech wandered to the west and settled in the hilly Bohemian countryside; Lech strayed northward and came upon a white eagle's nest. A ray of sunshine fell on its wings, making them appear tipped with gold. Lech took this as a good omen and decided to remain there. That eagle with a golden crown became the symbol of the Polish nation.

Lech named the place Gnieźno, a Polish word meaning nest. It served as the first capital of the Polish people. Lying not far from Poznań, it remains the birthplace of the Polish nation. But like Armagh, the ancient capital of Ireland, it never developed into much of a town. My Kowalski grandparents came from that region, which is referred to as Greater Poland (Wielkopolska).

My mother and her family, on the other hand, dwelled in what is known as Little Poland (Małopolska). Here the kings and noble figures of Polish history are buried on Wawel Hill in Cracow, the second capital. In this region also lies the famed national shrine of Our Lady at Częstochowa. But here alas the Nazis also imposed their notorious concentration camp, Auschwitz.

The modern history of Poland is engulfed in catastrophic tragedy. Neighbors to the east and the west united to annihilate the Polish state and enslave its people not just once, in the 1790s, but again in my lifetime, in 1939. I find it hard to comprehend that the perpetrators of these monstrous deeds were not Muslim terrorists nor primitive pagans, but cultured Christian neighbors.

The experience of the Polish people is not unlike that of the Chosen People during one of the darkest periods of Jewish history—the Sixth-Century BCE Babylonian Exile. The captives were totally helpless. Never again would they see the Holy Land. And yet in the midst of their chaos, Deutero-Isaiah preached a remarkable message of hope:

> "Comfort, comfort my people, says your God.
> Speak tenderly to Jerusalem, and cry to her
> that her warfare is ended, that her iniquity is pardoned,
> that she has received from the Lord's hand double for all
> her sins."
> (Isaiah 40:1–2)

I have learned that, in facing oppression, we must never respond in kind. That would sink us to the level of our tormentors and, if the tables are turned, might impel us to show the same disdain toward them. It would truly diminish us. We are noble human beings made in the image and likeness of God. We are objects of God's immense love, destined to manifest the same love toward others. Hatred must never divert us from that responsibility.

I am occasionally asked, "Do you hate the Germans?" Elie Wiesel, the distinguished Holocaust survivor, responded to that same question by saying, "I do not hate them. I do not believe in collective guilt. The children of killers are not killers." I cannot improve on that. When I look at my closest friends, I find about half of them are of German descent. And yet I am not aware of any manifestation of hate or even mistrust—either they toward me or I toward them. So I reject the very notion of getting even or revenge.

One of the most difficult tasks for me has been that of learning to deal with people who harbor a deep-seated hatred toward me. This has not happened often, but when it does, the realization is paralyzing. I feel helpless. But I have come to understand that bearing with such abuse is not without merit. Our Jewish brothers and sisters endured the same under demonic Nazis, Native Americans coped with the same under the Conquistadores, our black brothers and sisters dealt with the same for centuries, women have struggled with it in politics and religion, and members of the gay and lesbian community still face it daily.

One cannot reflect long on the history of the Polish people and the story of my family without deep feelings of solidarity with the oppressed of this earth. It could not be otherwise. The lessons are painted in blood and agony. Seeing the results of pure hatred has led me to a greater identification with the poor, the suffering, and the despised of this earth. It has also instilled in me a deeper admiration and appreciation for my beloved Polish sisters and brothers.

The white eagle, bloodied and abandoned, flies again. That symbol of a free Poland was restored during the Communist period but not allowed to be depicted with a royal crown. Such an image was deemed inconsistent with a socialist state. In the fall of 1989, however, the Polish people soundly rejected Communism. That year did not end before the Polish government proudly restored the ancient emblem of Poland, the crowned white eagle. May she rise again to ever greater heights!

ACKNOWLEDGEMENTS

I am deeply indebted to many people for assisting in the development of this book. First there is my brother, Tom, who accompanied me on some of these journeys, and my sister, Ronnie, the oldest of the remaining Kowalskis. Both have reviewed the text for accuracy of the family stories.

The review of Polish history and related matters was undertaken by my college classmate at Orchard Lake, Michigan, Art Wagner and his wife Maddy. Geographical and historical accuracy was also astutely analyzed by my Charlestown colleague, former CIA analyst and geographer, Joe Baclawski. Editorial expertise was superbly rendered by our good friend, Ann Reynolds, as well as the Wagners.

Many staffers at Ex Libris, including editors and marketing specialists, had a hand in bringing this book to the light of day. To each of them I am grateful.

Lastly, I will always be enormously indebted to my beloved wife, Joan, and our dear son, John, who provided the support and the leisure that enabled me to travel, record, and reflect on these marvelous stories which mean so much to me. To them I dedicate this book.

INDEX